St. John Island, USVI

Travel Guide, Vacation, Holiday, Honeymoon

Author
Paul Gibson

Copyright Notice

Table of Content

Touristic Introduction

About St John

St. John, the smallest & most idyllic of the three United States Virgin Islands, is best known for its dozens of post card perfect white sand beaches, turquoise bays abounding in colorful corals & rainbows of tropical fish & endless vistas of green velvet hills. Only nine miles long & three miles wide, two thirds of the island is the Virgin Islands National Park, so its spectacular beaches & untouched forests will remain that way for generations to come & be accessible to all. There are tours of the National Park by Jeep or safari bus & hikes on spectacular trails led by Park Rangers who enrich the experience with talks on the island's history & geology as well as its flora & fauna. Frequent visitors to St. John are beach lovers who aren't content to only read about St. John in books but are always ready to go back to the beach.

While it is only twenty minutes from St. Thomas by convenient hourly ferry, St. John is the peaceful, uncommercialized paradise of island fantasies. It has no high-rise buildings, cruise ship docks or airport. Visitors can obtain discounted air fares to St. Thomas.

Despite its unspoiled atmosphere, it offers every facility & amenity found at major resorts.

Watersports abound! One can charter boats from kayaks to ketches to catamarans by the day or week, with or without captain.   Day excursions for sightseeing, picnicking, snorkeling, or scuba diving are offered on every variety of sail or motor craft. Sport fishing in our waters is an experience you'll always remember. Activities on land include hikes you can take on your own or with a National Park guide, horseback riding, donkey trail rides, rock climbing, exploring historic ruins & more.

Getting around the island is easy. Cruz Bay, the major town where the ferry docks, is on the west end of the island facing Red Hook in St. Thomas. It is connected by well maintained paved roads (see map) to most of the bays & beaches & to Coral Bay, the picturesque yacht harbor on the east end of the island. Several local agencies, all a short walk from the ferry dock, offer rental cars, jeeps & canopied trucks by the day or week. Colorful canopied taxis also line the dock all day & evening, offering rides to every island destination & tours.

The spectrum of accommodations offered at every budget level include two luxury resort hotels, privately owned million dollar villas & private vacation homes with million dollar views, sophisticated condominium apartments, guest houses & small inns with lots of atmosphere & campsites in the National Park.

Most of the private homes & condominiums are managed by professional property managers who live on the island & can give complete information including brochures on their properties & assist in finding a property which meets a visitor's requirements.

St. John's surprisingly large selection of restaurants runs from breeze cooled spots for barbecue or burgers to air-conditioned hideaways for Continental cuisine & candlelight. There are many great chefs cooking on the island. The hotels, restaurants & bars offer evening entertainment by the great array of talented, world-class musicians that St. John attracts.

Visitors who have rented homes or condos find ample supplies of fresh & frozen foods, delicatessen & baked goods & a good selection of liquors & wines.

For vacationers staying on St. John or day trippers from St. Thomas or cruise ships, shopping on St. John is a pleasant surprise, whether for luxuries or necessities. Instead of the cheap T-shirt stops which plague so many resorts, St. John offers imaginative shops with distinctive resort wear, quality jewelry, unique international & local crafts & duty free luxury goods. The island is home to many talented artists who work in a wide array of mediums & modes. Meet them & see their work at the island's art galleries & artists' studios. Take home a made-on-St. John work of art that can bring back the island feeling every time you look at it. St. John's three shopping areas, all within walking distance of the ferry & each with a personality all its own, are attractions in themselves offering charming restaurants, cafes & bars along with the shops.

Just being on St. John promotes health & wellness. Take it a step further & pamper, groom, work out, adjust, sweat, revitalize, integrate, renew, beautify or refresh yourself while you visit. What if you get too much sun? Or maybe you would like to know about the medical resources on St. John, just in case. Our island has that covered too.

Special situations are easily handled. When you would like to send a fax, check your e-mail, fill a prescription, find a newspaper, or need other helpful services, St. John probably offers just what you need.

Always inspiring, St. John has been written about from every angle & many books tell tales of fact & fiction, suggest things to do & reveal its hidden treasures.

Maybe you have already fallen in love with St. John and would like to explore the possibility of owning your own home, villa, or condominium on this beautiful island. Our real estate companies will be happy to discuss the possibilities. They can also show you home sites of many varieties. Whether you are considering building your cottage on the beach or your dream house, you will want to work with experienced local professionals. The island's architects, designers & builders can discuss with you, the special joys of construction in a tropical paradise & work with you to make your vision a reality.

Maybe you have fallen in love with each other & would like to know more about weddings on St. John. A perfect ceremony & celebration in paradise, as simple or elaborate as you wish, is an island specialty. Our many charming houses of worshipwould be happy to see you at your nuptials or at any service during your visit.

Most people who visit, come back again & again. And are always welcome!

History

Archaeological evidence suggests that Indians inhabited St. John as early as 770 BC, however there were no lasting settlements until the 1720s. Attracted by the possibility of cultivating sugar cane for profit, several European countries laid claim to the little island around that time.

The British had claimed St. John when the Danish government took possession in 1684. Although the British had no settlement on St. John, residents on Tortola considered the island to be theirs. The first party of Danes that tried to settle St. John was asked to leave. The two countries disputed over ownership for some time.

On March 25th, 1718 a group of Danish planters from St. Thomas raised their flag at the first permanent settlement at Estate Carolina in Coral Bay. The group is said to have included 20 settlers. Coral Bay was not the finest area for planting but it had an excellent natural harbor. At this time the Danish colony on St. Thomas was well established and Danish and Dutch planters were excited by the prospects of establishing plantations on St. John.

The British continued their attempts to overtake the Danes on St. John, however in 1762, to keep good relations with the Danes they finally relinquished their claims. Expansion happened quickly. In 15 years approximately 109 cotton and sugar cane plantations covered almost all of St. John.

Plantation life

St. John's hilly terrain meant that it was a must that the hills be cleared and terraced. The soil became thin when the trees were cleared; this made it necessary to add ashes and dung to the soil to maintain fertility.

Sugar cane had to be cultivated and processed. The growing number of plantations created a need for labor. It was not profitable to hire workers for the plantations. African slaves and indentured servants were brought to St. John to work the plantations. It was not long before the number of slaves on the island hugely outnumbered free-men.

Revolt of 1733

In 1733 there was a revolt on St. John against plantation owners and against slavery. On November 23rd, about 14 slaves entered Fortsberg with cane knives hidden in bundles of wood. They killed 6 out of 7 men in the garrison, took over the fort and fired one cannon to signal to the other slaves that the revolt had begun. The events that lead up to the revolt included; the adoption of a harsh slave code, the arrival of an elite group of African tribal rulers who preferred death to life as slaves and a summer of natural disasters, including a drought, two hurricanes, insect plaque and the possibility of famine. The seven month revolt left many Europeans and Africans dead.

The recorded population at the time of the revolt was 1,295 – 1,087 slaves and 208 freemen. These figures do not include children under twelve or people who worked on company plantations in Coral Bay. The true population therefore was greater than 1,295. During the revolt almost a quarter of the island's population was killed and large plantations were destroyed. Many slaves killed themselves when they thought the soldiers were going to capture them. French and Swiss soldiers from a neighboring island came to the aid of the Danes and settled the revolt.

In 1825 the Danish government opened a new courthouse and prison in Cruz Bay. The structure was intended to improve the treatment of slaves on St. John, by making justice a government issue rather than leaving it to individual planters. This building is now known as the Battery and is the only government building from the Danish Colonial period that remains.

Slavery Abolished

The Danish Parliament around this time created a 12-year plan where slavery would be slowly dissolved. Many slaves said they would not wait 12 years. A revolt on St. Croix prompted Governor General Peter Von Scholten on July 3rd, 1848 to abandon the Parliament's plan and abolished slavery in the Danish West Indies.

With the end of slavery came the decline of St. John's plantations and a dramatic drop in population. Between 1850 and 1870 St. John is said to have lost half its population. The plantation at Carolina Estate was kept running the longest by use of bay oil and cattle, and the Reef Bay continued operation until 1919 as it had been converted to steam power. As sugar production became profitless, bankrupt planters abandoned the island and former slaves moved onto the land. Some bought the land, others were given land gifts from former owners and the remainder became squatters.

The main economy of St. John for many years following the decline of plantation life was small scale subsistence farming. The island saw prospects of renewed sugar economy when in the 1870's the possibility of producing cheaper sugar with beets was considered. However this did not happen, as St. Croix and Puerto Rico were able to produce sugar more effectively and for less money. The island was left to the inhabitant that lived off the land and sea. Around 1913 the population of St. John is said to have been about 930 persons.

United States Virgin Islands

In 1917 the United States bought St. John from Denmark. By the 1930's, news of the beautiful American island had spread to the United States mainland and the beginning of what was to become a tourism boom on St. John was established.

Laurence Rockefeller in 1956 donated land to the Federal Government to establish a National Park. The 5000 acres became the nation's twenty-ninth National Park. The land was presented to Fred Seaton, who was the Secretary of the Interior, he promised the government would 'take good and proper care of these precious acres and verdant hills and valleys and miles of sunny, sandy shores'. Since then other donations have been made and presently the Virgin Islands National Park includes 7200 acres of land and 5600 acres of underwater lands.

Today St. John thrives as a favored tourist destination. A construction boom in the past couple of years is changing St. John from a quiet, sleepy island to one with a little more traffic and development

Travel and Tourism

The best way to see St. John quickly, especially if you're on a cruise-ship layover, is to take a 2-hour taxi tour. The cost is $25 per person. Almost any taxi at Cruz Bay will take you on these tours, or you can call the St. John Taxi Association (tel. 340/693-7530).

Many visitors spend time at Cruz Bay, where the ferry docks. This village has interesting bars, restaurants, boutiques, and pastel-painted houses. It's a bit sleepy, but relaxing after the fast pace of St. Thomas.

Much of the island is taken up with the Virgin Islands National Park (tel. 340/776-6201), with the lushest concentration of flora and fauna in the U.S. Virgin Islands. The park totals 12,624 acres, including submerged lands and water adjacent to St. John, and has more than 20 miles of hiking trails to explore. From pelicans to sandpipers, from mahogany to bay trees, the park abounds in beauty, including a burst of tropical flowers such as the tamarind and the flamboyant. The mongoose also calls it home. Park guides lead nature walks through this park that often take you past ruins of former plantations.

Other major sights on the island include Trunk Bay, one of the world's most beautiful beaches, and Fort Berg (also called Fortsberg), at Coral Bay, which served as the base for the soldiers who brutally crushed the 1733 slave revolt. Finally, try to make time for the Annaberg Sugar Plantation Ruins on Leinster Bay Road, where the Danes maintained a thriving plantation and sugar mill after 1718. It's located off Northshore Road, east of Trunk Bay. Admission is free. On certain days of the week (dates vary), guided walks of the area are given by park rangers.

Attraction

Attractions on St. John, Virgin Islands

The incredible beauty of St. John will leave you breathless. The entire island, from the forested hills to the glistening sapphire waters, is a treasure. Protecting a large portion of this natural beauty is the Virgin Islands National Park. The park is St. John's biggest attraction. It includes dozens of hiking trails, gorgeous beaches and historic ruins. Interpretive lectures and activities are available through the park service; and you can easily explore on your own. One road runs across the center of the island and another along the north shore. Driving and hiking around the island will lead you through lush forest, over mountaintops and along lovely coastlines and beaches.

Virgin Islands National Park

The Virgin Islands National Park on St. John encompasses miles of lush forest, historic plantation ruins, pristine beaches and coral reefs teaming with marine life. Trails weave by scenic lookout points, many ending at the shoreline of a wonderful beach. Sun seekers will be delighted by the beaches on St. John, which are some of the most beautiful in the Caribbean. The park is well developed which makes exploring the historical sites, beaches and trails easy and rewarding. The top points of interest are Trunk Bay, Cinnamon Bay, Cinnamon Bay Plantation ruins and Annaberg Plantation. These are just four of the dozens of beautiful areas you can explore. You can enjoy the National Park by boat, camping, fishing, kayaking, hiking, scuba diving, snorkeling, swimming and bird watching!

Brief History of the Park

In 1956 Lawrence Rockefeller, through the non-profit organization Jackson Hole Inc., donated 5000 acres of land on St. John to the National Park Service. On August 2nd of the same year United States Congress passed legislation to establish the Virgin Islands

National Park. The legislation stipulated that the Park's holdings on St. John could not exceed 9,485 acres. St. John contains a total of 12,500 acres. In 1962 the boundaries of the Virgin Islands National Park were expanded to include 5,650 acres of submerged lands and waters that contain a significant amount of coral reefs, shorelines and marine life.

In 2001 the Virgin Islands Coral Reef National Monument was established from 12,708 acres of federally owned submerged lands off the island of St. John. This area, administered by the National Park Service, protects coral reef and mangrove habitat crucial for the biological diversity of the entire Caribbean.

In 1978 a large portion of Hassel Island, a small island within St. Thomas' Charlotte Amalie Harbor, was donated to the Virgin Islands National Park.

Hassel Island

Hassel Island is 135 acres in size of which 122 acres are part of the Virgin Islands National Park. Once a peninsula connected to St. Thomas, the land mass was separated in 1860 by the Danish Government in order to facilitate better water and vessel circulation in the Charlotte Amalie harbor. There are four historical structures on the island now listed on the National Historic Places Registry. One of these structures is the remains of a British military garrison built during a brief British occupation of the former Danish West Indies (what is today the US Virgin Islands) in the 1800s. Another historical site is the Creque Marine Railway which dates back to the mid-1800s and is one of the oldest surviving examples of such a railway.

Virgin Islands National Park

1300 Cruz Bay Creek

St. John, VI 00830

Telephone: (340) 776-6201

General Park Admission: Free.

Trunk Bay Fee: $4 Adults, 16 and under, no charge. Golden Age & Golden Access annual card holders, 1/2 price.

Annual fees: $10 individual, $15 family.

Donations accepted at the Cruz Bay Visitor Center.

Activities in the VI National Park, St. John

The Virgin Islands National Park's diverse beaches, coral reefs, historic ruins and hiking trails provide endless hours of exploration and enjoyment, as well as inspiration and opportunities for reflection. Visitors can enjoy a variety of activities on the land and in the water. Some visitors explore the park on their own, while others prefer a guided tour with a park sponsored program, a boat charter or by taxi.

Beaches

Beautiful beaches are definitely a large factor in the allure of the Virgin Islands National Park. White sand, crystal clear water, great snorkeling, sunny warm climate and the tranquility of St. John lends to an unforgettable experience. The most well known of St. John's beaches is with out a doubt Trunk Bay; voted most beautiful, most photographed and is just overall a great beach. Cinnamon Bay is another very popular beach as is Caneel Bay, Hawksnest, Honeymoon and Maho Bay just to name a few. There are many beach options. Visit the St. John Beach Guide to help you decide.

Snorkeling

The marine environment in the National Park's waters are incredible. Coral reefs, sea fans, small and large fish, rays, turtles are all there for you to behold and appreciate. Trunk Bay has a 225-yard, self-guiding snorkeling trail marked by underwater signs that identify coral and marine life. Other beach accessible snorkeling sites are available like Waterlemon Cay, Lameshur and Caneel Bay. Visit: St. John Snorkeling

Diving

The Virgin Islands ranks as one of the Caribbean's premier diving sites. Some major points of interest include Whistling Cay, Haulover Bay and Reef Bay. For the safety of yourself and others, scuba diving is not permitted off designated swim beaches. Dive operators on St. John are available to rent gear from, teach introductory dive classes, certify and take you out diving! Visit: St. John Snorkeling

Hiking

There are 22 unique nature trails in the National Park, you are bound to find several that appeal to you. You can find an enjoyable 30 minute stroll through shady trees or an invigorating full day hike through Danish plantation ruins, mysterious carvings and lush forest. Which ever you choose you will be taken away by the beauty of the Virgin Islands National Park!

Special National Park Tours and Demonstrations

Contact the Visitor Center at (340) 776-6201, ext. 238 to inquire and make reservations for the special National Park interpretative programs listed below:

Annaberg Cultural History Demonstration

Visit Annaberg Sugar Plantation ruins and learn about sugar production, the slave trade during the period of European economic expansion in the West Indies and what former slaves did to survive after emancipation. Witness bread-baking on a coal pot, basket weaving and subsistence gardening demonstrations. Activities begin at 10:00 am and end at 2:00 pm on Tuesdays and Wednesdays for basket weaving, Wednesdays thru

Fridays for bread baking and Tuesdays thru Fridays for gardening.

Snorkel Trip

Tuesdays at 9:30 am. Snorkel over a coral reef and discover the Parks underwater treasures. The ranger will point out different coral formations, the organisms that live there and explain how they relate to each other. In addition, you will learn what the Park is doing to protect these valuable resources. Bring your mask, snorkel, fins and a t-shirt to prevent sunburn. Program is not for novice snorkelers. Meet at Trunk Bay's west lifeguard stand.

Waters Edge Walk

Sundays at 10:30 am. Where the land meets the sea you will find the shoreline, a place of constant environmental change. Many plants and animals depend on this complex zone for their survival. For example, ghost crabs inhabit the white sand beaches scavenging for food, and mangroves provide shelter and protection for juvenile fish and crustaceans. Join a ranger and learn more about the coastal plants and animals. Meet at the Leinster Bay trail head below the Annaberg ruins. Shoes for wading are recommended.

Evening Program

Mondays at 7:30 pm, Cinnamon Bay Campground Amphitheater. (Except in September when campgrounds are closed.) The Evening Programs, entitled "A Ranger's Choice", include slide shows, talks or demonstrations on different topics about the Park and the island of St. John. Program topics include the flora, fauna, history and culture.

Reef Bay Hike

Every Monday and Thursday, at 9:30 am; schedule is subject to change based on demand. Space is limited. The secrets of St. John's tropical forest, petroglyphs, and sugar mill ruins come alive on this three-mile hike.

The hike is mostly downhill, but is not necessarily easy due to its length, steep rocky terrain, short but strenuous uphill sections, and the prevailing heat and humidity. In addition, there is the remote possibility that deteriorating sea conditions might require hiking back uphill to the trail head. Visitors with circulatory or joint/muscle problems, other medical conditions, or with small children, should carefully evaluate their ability to do this hike. This hike includes transportation: a shuttle ride to the trail head (cost $5.00) and a boat pick-up which returns hikers to the Visitor Center (cost $15.00). All hikers must meet at the Visitor Center by 9:30 am. Participants should bring lunch, 1 – 2 liters of water per person, any special medication (taken daily) and a swimsuit for a quick swim at the trails end. Wear good hiking shoes (no open-toed footwear or aqua socks) and cool comfortable clothing.

Boating

Renting a boat and beach hopping is a great experience. You can also charter a boat with captain for a day or a yacht for a week or more. There are rental boat operations on St. John that rent small boats and dinghies perfect for a day of beach hopping via the sea! Daysail charters will show you some of the beautiful shorelines and snorkeling areas of the National Park and often include lunch and drinks, making for a perfect and relaxing day.

Bird Watching

Bird watchers will enjoy hiking around St. John and in particular the Francis Bay trail. The winter months are the optimum time for bird watching. There are some 160 bird species known to the islands, including parrots, hummingbirds, pelicans, ducks, egrets and more. Contact the National Park Visitor Center about bird watching trips that they might offer.

Fishing

Fishing in Park waters is open only to hand held rods. No fishing is allowed in Trunk Bay or in any beach swimming areas. Spear guns are prohibited..

Camping

Camping on National Park lands on St. John is restricted to the Cinnamon Bay Campground. Accommodations include bare tent sites, sites with tent-covered platforms already set up and small cottages. No backcountry or beach camping is permitted within Virgin Islands National Park.

Archeological Research

The Virgin Islands National Park Archeological Lab is located at Cinnamon Bay. This lab is open to visitors, who may want to take a peak at recently discovered artifacts, learn more about the archeological history of the island or volunteer..

For Kids – Junior Ranger Program

To help protect the natural and cultural resources of St. John, you are welcomed to join the Junior Ranger program on St. John. Stop by the Visitor Center and pick up a Junior Ranger workbook. Workbook exercises include "interviews" with trees, word searches, games and a nature hike. At the end, you return to the Visitor Center and you are awarded with a Junior Ranger program certificate, "Smokey Bear" hat, Junior Ranger badge and pencil. This is a fun, educational activity for kids to do while visiting Virgin Islands National Park.

Scenic Drive or Tour

Several roads around St. John have roadside observation points or photo stops giving you panoramic views of Trunk Bay, Maho Bay, Caneel Bay, Coral Bay and others. Roads are well maintained but narrow and sometimes steep. Renting a car and exploring is lots of fun. For those that rather not rent a car taxi operators can show you around.

Parties, Weddings, Picnics

Special use permits are required for organized activities that include ten (10) or more people for events such as weddings, birthday parties, etc. Picnic pavilions and grills are available for all activities.

However you choose to explore the Virgin Islands National Park you will undoubtedly leave with unforgettable memories of St. John.

The Visitors' Center, in Cruz Bay, is the place to start your exploration of St. John. The exhibits presented will introduce you to the park's history, hiking trails, historical sites andlocal flora and fauna. Park rangers can help answer questions about trails and hikes. Brochures about the Park, maps and books are also available at the center. The center is open daily from 8 am to 4:30 pm.

Cruz Bay

The main "town" on St. John is Cruz Bay. It's the arrival place for ferries from St. Thomas, its home to the post office and government offices, and it's a center for shopping, eating, drinking and being merry! Cruz Bay's nickname is Love City; earned because of its eclectic, take it easy vibe. While in Cruz Bay you can visit the National Park Visitor Center, stop into the Elaine Sprauve Library (housed in the 1750's Estate Enighed House), grab a cool beverage and relax in Cruz Bay Park, or take leisurely stroll through the shops and restaurants.

Attractions in Cruz Bay

Annaberg Plantation

Annaberg Plantation, as of 1780, was one of 25 active sugar producing factories on St. John. Other products produced at Annaberg were molasses and rum. Annaberg was named after William Gottschalk's daughter and translates to Anna's Hill. Gottschalk was the plantation owner. Slave labor was used to clear densely forested hillsides and to terrace the slopes around Annaberg to make farming possible. Slave labor was also used to plant, harvest and process the sugarcane. When slavery was abolished, plantations were divided. The 518 acres that were once Annaberg Plantation were divided into smaller farms.

Today the plantation ruins are protected by the Virgin Islands National Park and are open to the public. Trees have reclaimed the hillsides around Annaberg. A trail leads through factory ruins, slave quarters, windmill and other remains. Placards and signs along the trails describe how sugar was produced and discuss plantation life and the history behind sugar plantations on St. John and in particular Annaberg.

The windmill at Annaberg, one of focal points of the site, was built possibly between 1810 and 1830, and was one of the largest in the islands. Thirty four feet in diameter at the base and twenty feet at the top, the mill stands thirty eight feet high. When there was no wind to work the windmill, a horse mill would be used. The horses or mules were plodded in a circular motion; this turned the upright rollers in the center of the platform. Slaves passed cane stalk through the rollers and a box at the bottom caught the juice. The juice ran by gravity through gutters to the factory for processing. Three to five hundred gallons of juice could be produced in an hour.

The cane juice flowed first into a large copper kettle, where a fire was lit beneath. The excess water evaporated and workers would ladle the juice from one kettle to the next, down a line of five kettles. The juice eventually became concentrated through various levels of heating and evaporation. The concentrated juice was then placed in a box to crystallize. The crystallized brown sugar was then put in barrels that held up to 1,600 pounds of sugar. Early removal from the last heated kettle prevented crystals from forming however produced molasses that was used to make rum.

Some of the heating kettles used in the process described above are visible at Annaberg in the building photographed on the right.

Evidence of about 16 slave cabins were found in the Annaberg area. The construction of the cabins consisted of branches woven together with lime and a mud mixture. The roofs were likely made of palm leaves. The cabins deteriorated over time and are not fully standing; placards do indicate where the cabins were located and describe them.

Educational Center and Archaeology Laboratory at Cinnamon Bay

The Educational Center and Archaeology Laboratory at Cinnamon Bay, also called the Cinnamon Bay Museum, houses exhibits that chronicle the known human occupation of the islands from approximately 3,000 years ago to the founding of the park in the 1950s and are based on information gathered from archaeological sites and archaeological finds in the Virgin Islands. The Center focuses on discoveries made within Virgin Islands National Park. It is a working archeology lab and museum with the purpose of preserving the Caribbean's human heritage from prehistory to the present. The museum has been designed for teachers to utilize its unique exhibits to help local students learn and explore their heritage, as well as educate visitors about the significant role these islands played in maritime history. Researchers and interns also utilize the space as a working laboratory. The center is housed in one of the oldest still standing and in use buildings on St. John. The museum is volunteer run, and is generally open weekdays from 9am to 4pm. To double check hours of operation and for more information call: (340) 715-8580.

Elaine I. Sprauve Public Library

Elaine Ione Sprauve Public Library is located just outside of Cruz Bay. In addition to books, the library's collection includes interesting old photographs of St. John, newspaper clippings and paintings. The library is housed in the restored Enighed Estate House (pronounced en-nee-high). Visiting the library is a wonderful opportunity to explore one of the first substantial buildings of its kind on St. John. The plantation greathouse dates to 1757. The earliest recorded owner was the Wood family. A gravestone located in the family cemetery next to the greathouse/library indicates that a

William Wood died on the plantation estate on April 9, 1751. The estate and house change hands multiple times over the century. In the early 1900's a fire destroyed the greathouse. The burnt out shell, a shadow of its former beauty, would remain in this ruins for decades. On July 1, 1976 the site was admitted to the National Register of Historic Places; and by 1977 there was discussion of restoration. In 1980, with the restoration complete, the Enighed Estate House was renamed the Elaine Ione Sprauve Library and Museum of Cultural Arts – in honor of Sprauve's service to the government and contributions to the people of the Virgin Islands. Today the facility no longer includes the Museum of Cultural Arts. The Elaine I. Sprauve Public Library is operated by the Virgin Islands Division of Libraries, Archives and Museum. The library is open Monday through Friday from 9am to 1pm, and 2pm to 5pm (they are close between 1pm and 2pm). For more information call: (340) 776-6359.

Activities Guide

St. John is a picturesque little island that offers nature lovers an array of activities to partake in. One of the most popular activities is going to the beach, and that makes perfect sense considering many of the islands' fine sandy shorelines are protected by the National Park Service. For those interested in beach hoping visit the Beach Guide. An Attraction Guide and Shopping Guide are also available.

St. John offers rest, relaxation and an adequate amount of sporting activities. Plan the activities you would like to do most and have a great vacation!

St. John: Sailing Charters & Excursions

Sailing in the Caribbean breeze, over clear blue water, past lush green mountains... is there any image more representative of a vacation day in the Virgin Islands? Going on a sailing charter is a favorite activity during a St. John visit. The USVI are well known for sailing; the weather and scenery offer perfect conditions. Many captains have sailing stories from their Caribbean and world travels that entertain. Go sailing; delight in the wonderful weather, beautiful waters, and the service of professional and knowledgeable captains and crew members. Sailing charters are available in half day trips and full day. Amenities vary but very often include open bar, lunch, snorkel gear, floats, and other water toys. Sunset sails and dinner cruises are also an option. Enjoy the tranquil beauty of Caribbean evenings as the sun goes down and stars come out. Sitting on the deck of a sailboat watching the stars with a glass of wine is a lovely, romantic way to spend an evening. Visit the featured charters below for more information on what they offer!

Goddess Athena

Visit: www.sailusvi.com

Contact or Call (340) 277-3532

Join us for unique adventures aboard our stunning, one-of-a-kind pirate ship! Queen of the Fleet for over 40 years, her 84 feet of classic lines make Goddess Athena a sight to behold. Friendly, knowledgeable crew, wonderful food and drinks, and sailing/snorkeling excursions tailored to your tastes will provide memories to last a lifetime. We invite you to experience the magic of sailing as only the pirates of the Caribbean knew. Our record 100% guest satisfaction speaks volumes. Join us today aboard the Goddess! Cannons by Request. Busty Wenches by Appointment Only. Sailing from Cruz Bay, St John

Scubadu

Visit: www.sailvi.com

Contact or Call (340) 643-5155

Scubadu is a 43 by 25 foot luxury Catamaran, specializing in private day, sunset, and/or dinner sailing excursions. Leave the crowds behind as you explore the beautiful waters, islands, and beaches of the U.S. Virgin Islands. We sail to beautiful snorkel and swimming spots you can't get to by car. Scubadu departs from Cruz Bay, St. John or Red Hook, St.

Thomas. Because we only do private charters for a maximum of 12 people, we can customize your trip to your groups' needs. We provide the Captain, first mate, delicious food, beverages, snorkel gear, and fresh water showers. All you need to bring are towels and non-spray sunscreen

Catania Yacht Charters

Visit: www.cataniayachtcharters.com

Contact or Call (340) 514-1231

Come Sailing with Catania Yacht Charters: excursions in the USVI and BVI, specializing in small groups of up to 6 guests. Catania is a traditional 80 year old sloop with a legacy of spending over 30 years circumnavigating the globe. Be pampered on an unforgettable excursion of a lifetime. Captain Ocean will enthrall you with the history of the Virgin Islands and stories of his around the world voyage. Discover pristine white sand beaches and enchanting hidden coves. Experience an underwater world full of spectacular marine life. Enjoy refreshments from our open bar. Full day, half day, and sunset sails available.

St. John offers rest, relaxation and an adequate amount of sporting activities. Plan the activities you would like to do most and have a great vacation!

St. John: Eco-Tours & Park Adventures

The Virgin Islands National Park's beaches, coral reefs, historic ruins and hiking trails provide endless hours of exploration and enjoyment on St. John, as well as inspiration and opportunities for reflection. Visitors can enjoy a variety of activities on the land and in the water. Some visitors explore the park on their own, while others prefer a guided tour.

Eco-Tours

St. John is home to the Virgin Islands National Park which preserves about 3/4ths of the islands forest, it also includes thousands of acres of submerged lands and waters that contain a significant amount of coral reefs, shorelines and marine life. What better way to enjoy, understand and appreciate the rich natural and historical elements protected by the National Park than with expert guides to lead the way.

Virgin Islands Ecotours

Visit: viecotours.com

Contact or Call (877) 845-2925 (340) 779-2155

Every year Virgin Islands EcoTours receives Best of Awards such as: Kayak Tours, The Best EcoTour and Best Attraction by the readers of the VI Daily News. Kayak Hike & Snorkel Adventures are offered at three locations: St. Thomas Mangrove Lagoon; St. John Honeymoon Beach; and Historic Hassel Island. Professional guides lead ecological and historical tours where you kayak, hike and snorkel in one unforgettable adventure of fun and learning. VI

EcoTours received the Certificate of Excellence by Trip Advisor. Wedding, corporate and private groups receive personalized service. Book online or call toll free.

Guided Walking & Hiking Tours

Take a walking or hiking tour in the National Park with a professional and knowledgeable guide and learn about the islands history and ecology.

The National Park Service offers a guided hike of Reef Bay Trail. It is lead by a ranger and is a popular choice. It takes place every Monday and Thursday at 9:30 am. The schedule is subject to change based on demand. Enjoy learning about the secrets of St. John's tropical forest, petroglyphs and sugar mill ruins on this three-mile hike. Reservations are strongly recommended as space is limited. Contact the National Park Visitor's Center on St. John for more information.

You can explore the trails within the National Park on your own as well. Visit the National Park Trails section for more information.

St. John offers rest, relaxation and an adequate amount of sporting activities. Plan the activities you would like to do most and have a great vacation!

St. John offers rest, relaxation and an adequate amount of sporting activities. Plan the activities you would like to do most and have a great vacation!

St. John: Powerboat Rentals & Charters

Ask a visitor or resident what they love most about St. John and the list is likely to include the ocean, beaches, National Park, snorkeling, beautiful coastlines, tropical weather, and relaxing at a beach bar, toes in the sand, sipping a rum-drink. Looking for a fantastic way to get all of that into one perfect day? Go Boating! Boating is one of the highlights of a vacation to St. John. Visit the boat charters listed below for more information. Let them know whether your group is looking for party-time with your besties, a family vacation, a special wedding outing, or if you are looking for a luxury, exclusive excursion. Also, give them an idea of where you'd like to go, they of course will make suggestions too based on their knowledge of the area. At the end of this page is a section on What to Expect; it covers types of boats, rates, captain, fuel, and other details. Start planning what's likely to be the best day of your vacation to St. John, your day out boating.

Aqua Blue Charters

Visit: www.aquabluevi.com

Contact or Call (340) 344-1190

Aqua Blue Charters is owner-operated, so we can provide you personalized service for your best day of island hopping in the BVI and USVI. Create your itinerary with your private captain and tour guide before your trip. From snorkeling in St. John and the Indians, lunch at the Willy T or on Jost Van Dyke to sipping afternoon drinks at Soggy Dollar, the day is yours. We believe our expert knowledge of the best cruising area in the world will exceed all of your expectations. Our boat Mojo, comes with snorkeling gear, drinking water, ice, tons of shade and bean bag chairs to provide the most comfortable ride possible.

See and Ski Powerboat Rentals

Visit: www.seeski.com

Contact or Call (866) 775-6268 (340) 775-6265

See and Ski is the choice for chartering a boat by the St. Thomas/St. John community. The fleet features 26' Prowler Cats, powered by fuel efficient and reliable engines, equipped with full biminis for extensive shade coverage, coolers, ample dry storage and freshwater showers for your comfort. Known for their smooth, dry ride, the twin hulls take all sea conditions easily. Island

Hop, Beach Bar it, Fish, Dive, Spearfish or Snorkel. Checkout is streamlined. Your itinerary is individual to make it your day! Best Captains in the VI - experienced, knowledgeable & FUN! Explore, play, see & ski, the beauty of the Virgin Islands!

New Horizons II

Visit: www.newhorizonscharters.com

Contact or Call (800) 808-7604 (340) 775-1171

Explore the British Virgin Islands aboard a large comfortable powerboat " New Horizons II". Visit the Baths at Virgin Gorda, Guana Island for snorkeling at spectacular reefs, Marina Cay for Lunch, Jost Van Dyke and Soggy Dollar Bar. Enjoy breathtaking scenery on route and be entertained by our captain and crew's pirate stories and tales of island life. This excursion provides you with an open bar all day. Snorkeling equipment and Snorkel instruction are available. New

Horizons II sets sail daily. Reservations are required. We hope to hear from you soon.

Love City Excursions

Visit: www.lovecityexcursions.com

Contact or Call (340) 998-7604

Enjoy the best day of your vacation onboard CatZilla; Love City Excursions' roomy and comfortable world cat power catamaran. On your own private power boat you will snorkel in some of the world's clearest waters, and sip on delicious beverages while beach and bar hopping through our Caribbean Islands. Legally rated to hold 12 passengers and featuring two large coolers, bottled water, painkillers (local rum drink,) snorkeling gear, pool noodles, and comfortable bean bag chairs; CatZilla is the perfect boat for adults and children alike.

Beach Bum Boat Rentals

Visit: BeachBumBoatRentals.com

Contact or Call (855) 550-8728

Don't just "rent a boat"... have the best day of your vacation! We have the largest selection and widest variety of stylish and comfortable boats for rent on St Thomas & St John. Large group? We can accommodate up to 32 people on one boat! Swim with turtles, rays and dolphin, lay on white sand beaches, sip a Painkiller in a hammock at the Soggy Dollar Bar, and enjoy the spectacular beaches of the U.S. & British Virgin Islands. Your captain will customize the perfect day for you. Flexible cruise ship schedules. Reserve your day early, we book up fast!

Caribbean Blue Boat Charters

Visit: www.boatrentalsvi.com

Contact or Call (340) 690-2583

AFFORDABLE PRICING for Families & Friends! Rent a Private Boat w/Captain! Our Stylish 36ft Marlins provide a most comfortable ride. Feel the wind as you cruise the islands. Listen to Buffet, Reggae or your choice from our 12 speaker surround sound. Your Day, Your Way! Snorkel w/ turtles, rays & tropical fish. Explore around St. John, visit The Baths, Virgin Gorda, Jost Van Dyke, Willy T's or relax on a beautiful beach. Call us today to help design an unforgettable trip! All things are possible! Includes seating up to 12ppl, snorkel gear & bathroom. Our Captains are FUN & experienced. Visit TripAdvisor/Facebook. Call or Text, we book up fast!

Sonic Charters

Visit: www.sonicchartersstthomas.com

Contact or Call (340) 244-5096 (203) 889-6003

Sonic Charters offers private, custom day trips to the U.S. and British Virgin Islands on 32' Intrepid and 33' Jupiter center console powerboats. We also offer a 50' Sea Ray for a more luxurious experience. Whether you want to party the day away or lay back and unwind, we want to make it happen! With comfortable seating for up to 9 and capacity up to 12, Sonic Charters can provide unsurpassed luxury for a fun filled day. The USVI and BVI are an open canvas to explore; our local captains can take you to places other companies won't! We look forward to spending the day with you!

Island Flyer Catamaran Charters

Visit: www.islandflyercatamarancharters.com

Contact or Call (904) 504-6225

Island Flyer is a U.S. Coast Guard Inspected 36' catamaran certified to for up to 12 passengers. The ride is super smooth with plenty of room in the sun or shade. There is a head and private changing area with room below to store your things. Just a big fun boat. Captain and fuel are included! Beer, rum drinks, sodas and water are complementary. Private charters for small groups. Explore the USVI and BVI's. Choose your own itinerary. Call us, tell us what you would like to do, and we'll make it happen! We're all about customer service. We're here to make your trip memorable!

One Love Charters

Visit: www.onelovecharters.com

Contact or Call (340) 227-5229

Experience the British Virgin Islands and the U.S. Virgin Islands the way the locals do! Book with One Love Charters and you'll be able to visit all the destinations the VI has to offer... Including the ones you can't read about! Whether you want to snorkel beautiful reefs, bar hop beach to beach, or just relax on the boat with an ice cold beverage in hand, One Love Charters will work to make your day with us the highlight of your vacation!

Sunshine Daydream Charters

Visit: www.sunshinedaydreamvi.com

Contact or Call (340) 776-0928 (970) 708-4771

Come explore all the U.S. and British Virgin Islands

have to offer aboard Sunshine Daydream, your private ,owner-operated boat for the day. Snorkeling, island hopping, beach bars, shopping, whatever your pleasure let us show you the best day of your vacation! Sunshine Daydream offers spacious and comfortable seating in both the sun and shade for up to 8 guests, a large built in cooler stocked with ice and bottled water, top of the line Bluetooth sound system, swim noodles, and all the Coast Guard required safety gear to keep you and your loved ones safe while at sea.

Take It Easy

Visit: www.takeiteasyvi.com

Contact or Call (340) 677-1320

What do Brad Pitt, Kenny Chesney, and Cate Blanchett all have in common? They all cruised on Take it Easy! Explore the islands in luxury! Completely customizable charters around St. Thomas, St. John and the BVI; the day is yours! Whether it's with family, friends, a wedding party, or private getaway; you will surely enjoy the crystal blue waters and the warm Caribbean sun with TAKE IT EASY. Two luxurious Sea Rays available; accommodating 12 passengers each in comfort and style. Full bar and light snacks included. Learn more on our website, or at www.facebook.com/takeiteasyvi. Check out our excellent reviews on Trip Advisor!

Privateer Charters

Visit: www.privateercharters.com

Contact or Call (888) 727-0793

Full and Half Day Private US and British Virgin Islands Powerboat Charters. Spend the day with us and experience the beauty of St. John, the white sand beaches of Jost van Dyke, snorkel the Caves of Norman Island, or enjoy the Baths in Virgin Gorda! Let us help you create the perfect day. With over twenty years of professional nautical experience, Captain Patrick Cena prides himself on providing guests with comfortable, safe excursions that exceed their expectations. Parties of up to six will ride comfortably in our beautifully appointed 27' Everglades powerboat. For more information visit www.privateercharters.com or email info@privateercharters.com. For reservations please call 888-727-0793.

Rockhoppin' Charters

Visit: www.rockhoppin.com

Contact or Call (340) 626-2859 (340) 514-5527

Explore the USVI or BVIs on board of our comfortable 32 FS Regulator Powerboat with twin Yamaha 250s. It has cushioned, forward-facing seating and will provide a comfortable, dry ride. Join us on a day trip, half day trip or sunset cruise out of Cruz Bay, St. John. Our experienced Captains Steve and Tyler can take you anywhere in the USVI or BVI: Jost van Dyke, Norman Island, Willy T, Peter Island, Cooper Island, Tortola,

Virgin Gorda, Anegada... and will make sure you have a great day on the water. You can also use our new Easybreath Full Face Masks for free on your charter trip.

Lion In Da Sun

Visit: www.lionindasun.com

Contact or Call (340) 626-4783

Lion In Da Sun uses a 28ft Scout powerboat providing stability, speed, and open bow seating while island hopping on a day trip. Discover what the area is known for; snorkeling, beachside restaurants and bars and white sand beaches. Visit the BVI islands of Jost Van Dyke and Norman Island or head to the Baths for the day. Stay in U.S. waters and see all of what St. John has to offer in the bays and cays surrounding the island. Ultimately the entire trip is up to you; we are however more than pleased to help you design it and then boat you to the best day of your vacation!

Elixir Charters

Visit: www.elixircharters.com

Contact or Call (340) 344-3336

Elixir, a sixty foot custom Hatteras Motoryacht is the largest and finest day charter yacht in the Virgin Islands. Allow us to pamper you with an eggs benedict breakfast and filet mignon and lobster tail lunch served to you at a bronze sea turtle table on our shaded aft deck. Enjoy three fabulous snorkel/beachfront stops, top quality snorkel gear, double kayak, fast inflatable, double hammock, giant sun pad, air conditioned salon with Bose home theater system, and our open top shelf bar including vintage wine and champagne. Full day trips and sunset dinner cruises daily. BVI trips available on private charters. Unforgettable!

Island Roots Charters

Visit: www.IslandRootsCharters.com

Contact or Call (340) 643-5000

PRIVATE CHARTERS within your BUDGET! Knowledgeable local captains. Boats of varying size and price range. Guaranteed the BEST DAY of your vacation! FULL DAY trips starting as low as $450.

St. John Boat Rental

Visit: www.Stjohnboatrental.com

Contact or Call (340) 227-5144

Home of the $99 gas guarantee with the most professional crew in the islands. Pick from a variety of private charters boats legally certified for up to 12 passengers. We have boats for every budget starting at $450. Call for details (813) 465-2665 or visit stboat.com.

What to Expect: St. John Boat Rental and Charter Costs

There are a variety of options when it comes to boat rentals in St. John. Boats include 25'-35', 36'-44' to 45'-50'; and are center consoles, catamarans, or sport cruisers. Many boat charters cater to groups of 6, but several can accommodate 10 or 12 passengers. Prices vary by type of boat, size, capacity, and amenities. A half day charter on a center console averages $400-$600; and on a Sea Ray around $750-$900 for a half day. For a full day rental on a center console the range is $500-$1000; and full day on a Sea Ray about $1,300-$4,000. Meals are generally not included; some boats do have snacks and a few include ice, soft drinks, and water. You are welcome to bring your own or stop at a beachfront bar for lunch and refreshments.

Check whether the captain's fee is included in the rate or additional. Captain's rates are around $100 for half day, $150 for full day. Very few boat rentals are available bareboat; and the few that do require the renter to have strong knowledge of the area's waters. Fuel is another consideration; it is included in some boat rental rates, for others its additional based on usage. How much fuel is used is a factor of boat type and of distance traveled. Budget $75-$200 for fuel on a half day boat trip, and $150-$300 for a full day.

Want to head over to the British Virgin Islands on your boat trip? It belongs to another country; and there will be a custom's fee charges of around $45-$50 a person. If you explore and play within the U.S. Virgin Islands, then there are no additional fees related to customs. Gratuity is usually not included in the boat rental rates; and your captain and crew appreciate tips. All figures are provided for reference only, and are subject to change.

Parasailing on St. John

Get a bird's eye view of St. John's fabulous coastal scenery, green hillsides and the spectacular blue ocean that surrounds it all, with a fun parasailing adventure. From the excitement of that gentle lift off the boat into the sky; to soaring above it all attached to your colorful parachute – it's fun for the whole family. Go up in tandem with your sweetie or do a triple flight with your kids or friends. You will smile the whole time.

Parasail Virgin Islands

Visit: www.parasailstjohn.com

Contact or Call (340) 227-8303

Come fly with us in the beautiful U.S. Virgin Islands and experience the thrill of an Offshore Powerboat ride, Parachuting, Ballooning and Gliding all in one "Action Packed Adventure" at a fraction of the cost. We can accommodate ages 6 and up. With our 100% safety record, parasailing in St. Thomas and St. John is fun for the whole family!

St. John: Fishing

Anglers will have a terrific time testing their skill and trying their luck while fishing on vacation in St. John! Go offshore in pursuit of Marlin, Dolphin Fish (Mahi-

Mahi), Wahoo and Tuna. Or try inshore fishing and see whether you can get some Kingfish, Barracuda, Jacks or Yellowtail Snapper to bite!

Wondering if your big catch, the one you will be talking about for years to come, will be in season at the time of year you are planning your visit to St. John. The quick answer is that some species are around all year and others have peak seasons. Experienced fishing charter operators and captains in the area know the islands' waters and seasons. They can provide information on what you might find on the end of your line when you go out fishing with them during your St. John vacation.

Fishing charters on St. John offer trips that will excite everyone from the seasoned pro to the novice. They include inshore, offshore and marlin trips. Most operators offer trips lasting: ½ day (4 hours, typically between 8am and noon, or 1pm and 5pm); ¾ of a day

(6 hours); full day (8 hours); and Marlin trips (10 hours, usually 7:30am to dusk). Short trips are generally inshore fishing only. Boat capacity of 4 to 6 passengers is common. Rates for fishing charters varies depending on length of trip, size of boat, inclusion of fuel in the rate versus fuel being a surcharge, and differences in services and equipment provided. Fishing charters generally have the details of their trips listed on their websites, and can provide the information by email or telephone upon request. Explore your options; book a fishing trip and a have a great time

Are you looking forward to eating your catch? Guests can typically request some of their catch, for example up to 20 lbs, the remainder stays with the boat. If you are interested in keeping some of your catch to take back to your vacation villa to cook for dinner be sure to ask about it. If you are staying in a hotel, ask the captain for suggestions of restaurants on the island that will cook your catch for you!

If you are really a fishing enthusiast you might consider planning your vacation to St. John around a fishing tournament, to be a spectator or to participate! Some fishing charters are available for tournaments. You'll find various tournament options on neighboring St. Thomas, there aren't any hosted on St. John. Here is a sample: Couples Tournament (February), Dolphin Derby (April) and the USVI Open/Atlantic Blue Marlin Tournament (August).

St. John: Island Tours

St. John is well known for its beautiful vistas, beaches, lush forests, National Park and historical ruins. How do you take it all in is up to you. The most popular option is an island tour by taxi. You can also rent a car and do a self guided driving tour; or explore the main town on foot. Make the do-it-yourself tour easy by grabbing an activity and road map before heading out to explore.

St. John: Scuba Diving

The underwater world in the Virgin Islands is stunning and truly amazing! Explore corals and gorgonian forest of sea fans and sea whips. Dive around caves, explore sunken boat wrecks or take a night dive and explore the fantastic world of nocturnal marine life! Swim among turtles, bright parrotfish, blue tangs, schools of fry and so much more.

The marine environment around St. John is world class and there are world class dive operators here that can take you out for the first time, teach you to dive, get you certified and instruct you for higher levels of dive certification.

6-Paq Scuba

Visit: www.6paqscuba.com

Contact or Call (340) 626-7700

Art of Diving... Take your diving to a new level with our expert, Colette. 6800+ dives, 17+ years helping thousands comfortably dive St. John and surrounds. New or experienced, we help you master that buoyancy thing safely, with ease. Dive and Train. Privately: So we can focus just on YOU! Semi-privately: Share the dive, never more than 6. Now it's about balancing everyone's needs based on Seas. Dive like Astaire danced with Rodgers – Together we match our motion to the ocean. Let us help you or demonstrate you got it and privately play your day away your own way...

The best conditions for diving in the islands are found during the summer and fall months, with visibility generally between 60 and 100 feet. Some sites, particularly in Pillsbury Sound, can be explored all year round as they are protected from the wind and rough seas that can affect other more open sites during the winter months. St. John and St. Thomas are close enough to each other that they share many of the same dive sites in the Pillsbury Sound area including

Carval Rock, Congo Cay, Grass Cay, Mounds at Mingo, Arches and Tunnels of Thatch and Lovango Cay.

There are over a dozen dive sites around St. John. Most are shallow dives and many only 15 to 20 minutes away from the shore/dock. In addition to those located in the Pillsbury Sound other popular dive sites include Eagle Shoal, Flanagan Reef, Maple Leaf, Cocoloba and Witch's Hat.

Dive operators are familiar with the various dive locations and can safely guide you to and around them. An introductory course will run around $60 to $110. For the certified diver; two morning dives are around $95 and it is around $85 to $100 for a night dive. Certification course, $260-$400. Multi-day dive packages are also available. Whether you are a novice or a dive enthusiast, there is no better place to dive than in the warm, inviting waters around the Virgin Islands.

Scuba Diving Tips

➢ There is an excellent recompression chamber in the Schneider Regional Medical Center on St. Thomas. It is on 24 hours a day.

➢ Always check your equipment before each dive.

➢ Never dive alone.

➢ Enjoy the sites, but don't touch.

➢ The survival of the under water world depends largely on us; do not overturn rocks, kick up sand, pick up animals, touch coral. Be content with watching.

➢ Leave the underwater world as you found it; future divers and the marine life will be happy you did!

➢ Do not scuba dive if you are pregnant, too little is known about the effects of pressure on fetal development. Ask your doctor and/or dive professional for more information.

St. John offers rest, relaxation and an adequate amount of sporting activities. Plan the activities you would like to do most and have a great vacation!

St. John: Snorkeling & Snuba

Snorkeling

From new, never snorkeled before to seasoned snorkelers there is something for everyone. Rocky coast lines, near shore reefs, off shore cays and sunken items like ships and planes provide beautiful and varied snorkeling opportunities. The conditions are; great visibility, fairly constant water temperatures of 79-83 degrees year-round, calm seas with little current and fantastic underwater scenery. In other words, perfect for snorkeling. View gorgeous underwater gardens of coral and visit with the residents; turtles, rays, octopuses, moray eels and an abundance of fish large and small. With the use of a mask, snorkel and fins you can float on the surface and admire the marine life below. Snorkeling is an option from beaches and also by boat trips.

Eco Hike & Snorkel Tour: Lind Point to Honeymoon

Visit: viecotours.com

Contact or Call (877) 845-2925 (340) 779-2155

Explore the best of VI National Park above and below the water. Depart from the Visitor Center in Cruz Bay and hike the Lind Point Trail. Learn about flora, fauna, cultural and historical trivia along the way. At Honeymoon Beach your guide will teach you to snorkel and identify the colorful sea life. The final portion of your hike takes you through a grove of wild cinnamon, the botanical gardens of Caneel Bay Resort and the ruins of a Sugar Plantation. Perfect for wedding, corporate and private groups. Book online with Virgin Islands EcoTours or call toll free.

Best of Henley Cay and Caneel Bay Adventure

Visit: viecotours.rezgo.com

Contact or Call (877) 845-2925 (340) 779-2155

Enjoy the Best of Henley Cay and Caneel Bay Kayak, Hike & Snorkel Adventures "combined" into a 5 hour tour with a picnic lunch! Henley Cay is among St John's most colorful snorkeling destinations. See coral gardens, schools of tropical fishes and marine life at this deserted island. Seabirds soar overhead and feed nearby. Explore the Caneel Bay Peninsula. Kayak turquoise waters, hike Turtle Point Trail and snorkel to see turtles and sting rays. Look for deer, wild donkeys, mongoose and hermit crabs. Departs daily from Virgin Islands EcoTours' Honeymoon Beach Hut. Book online or call toll free

Caneel Bay Kayak, Hike & Snorkel Adventure

Visit: viecotours.rezgo.com

Contact or Call (877) 845-2925 (340) 779-2155

Listen to our guests! We are ranked #1 in Trip Advisor: "Best Experience on St. John", "Do it early in your trip", "Amazing Adventure", "Great family activity", "Learn and have fun exploring St. John!", "Very interactive tour of the islands unique ecology with a great staff.", "Don't miss this!". Kayak on turquoise waters, hike along scenic Turtle Point Trail and snorkel over coral reefs and see colorful fish, turtles and sting rays. Consider upgrading to a 5 hour tour with lunch: The Best of Henley Cay and Caneel Bay! Limited availability, reserve early. Book online or call us toll free.

Honeymoon Beach All-Inclusive Watersports Daypass

Visit: viecotours.com

Contact or Call (877) 845-2925 (340) 779-2155

Experience St John's most romantic beach with the All-Inclusive Day Pass; includes snorkel gear, life jacket, lounge chair, float, kayak, standup paddle board & locker. Relax in a hammock! Snorkel with sea turtles! Honeymoon Hut sells drinks & souvenirs with food available. Taxi to Caneel Bay Resort; then walk 8 minutes to Honeymoon Beach, or take a $5pp each way shuttle between the Caneel Bay parking and Honeymoon Beach. Another option, hike from Cruz Bay via Lind Point Trail to Honeymoon Beach. Perfect for wedding, corporate & private groups. $49 per adult. $10 per child. Book online using promo code VINOW for 10% discount or call toll free.

Henley Cay Kayak & Snorkel Adventure

Visit: viecotours.com

Contact or Call (877) 845-2925 (340) 779-2155

Henley Cay is one of St John's premier snorkeling spots! Kayakers and snorkelers love the challenge of a 20 minute paddle across Caneel Bay from Honeymoon Beach to Henley Cay, part of the VI National Park, a

UNESCO Biosphere Reserve. The protected beach is fringed with colorful coral reefs teeming with schools of vibrant fish and marine life. Flocks of seabirds fly overhead and feed close-by. Consider upgrading to a 5 hour tour with lunch: The Best of Henley Cay and Caneel Bay! Perfect for wedding, corporate and private groups. Book online using promo code VINOW for 10% discount or call us toll free.

Beach Guide

Rocky coast lines and near shore cays & reefs offer great opportunities to snorkel from beaches. Snorkeling from shore can be done with or without a guide.

St. John Snorkeling Favorites:

1.Trunk Bay

Beautiful waters and wonderful white sand has made picturesque Trunk Bay one of the most popular beaches on St. John. Renowned for it's underwater snorkeling trail, Trunk Bay is definitely worth a visit. Six hundred and fifty (650) feet of underwater trails are a highlight for Trunk Bay's visitors. You can rent snorkel gear on the beach. Trunk Bay is part of the National Park and is the only beach on St. John that has an admission fee. Fee is collected from 8am to 4pm. The beach is a popular stop on tour itineraries and can get very busy on days when there are several cruise ships in port on St. Thomas or anchored off of St. John. Trunk Bay has been voted one of the most photogenic beaches in the Caribbean. Lifeguards are on duty daily.

2.Cinnamon Bay

Cinnamon Bay, at about 1 mile, is the National Park's longest beach. This great beach offers snorkeling, swimming, volleyball and more. A watersports concession stand rents windsurfing equipment, kayaks and mountain bikes. There is good snorkeling around Cinnamon Bay Cay, a short swim from shore. The clear waters will tempt you to spend your time swimming and snorkeling, while the palm trees will call you to spread your beach blanket in the shade and relax. Across from the beach and campground entrance/parking area is a Hiking Trail through the Cinnamon Bay Plantation ruins.

3.Leinster/Waterlemon Bay

Leinster Bay, is bordered by the Leinster Bay Trail. The area before the parking lot is great for walking and exploring. Mangrove trees line the left side of the bay. The water is very shallow for a distance and then it quickly drops off and becomes the open ocean. The shoreline is fairly pebbly, however there are a few sandy areas that can be used to enter the water for a swim. A 10-15 minute walk from the parking area down the trail will bring you to a narrow stretch of sand. Another 10 minutes down the trail is Waterlemon Bay, a lovely, often quiet beach. Waterlemon Cay, located a longish swim from shore, offers excellent snorkeling. Walking along the rocky coast on an unofficial trail to the tip of the bay will allow you to enter at a closer point to the cay for a shorter swim. A strong current runs along the back, right side of the cay, use caution.

4.Hawksnest

Hawknest, a National Park Beach, has gorgeous clear water and a pretty shoreline. A covered shed with picnic tables makes the beach a favorite with residents, particularly on weekends for picnics and in late afternoons for a relaxing swim after work. This beach has good parking and is easily accessed from the road. The beach is lined with sea grape trees that offer a bit of shade. A great beach for enjoying a few hours of perfect waters and sunshine!

5.Honeymoon Beach

Looking for a sun kissed stretch of sand to relax and revitalize, while also having the option to get active and explore. This is it. Honeymoon Beach is a pretty beach with sandy shoreline surrounded by sea grape and coconut trees. Hammocks and picnic tables are scattered under the trees. The crystal clear turquoise waters are rich in marine life and offer great snorkeling, particularly around the rocky headland that extends into the water between Honeymoon Beach and Solomon Bay next door.

You can access Honeymoon Beach via Lind Point Trail which starts just behind the Virgin Islands National Park Visitor Center in Cruz Bay and connects to Caneel Bay Resort, see our National Park trails page for more information. Or you can take a taxi, or drive and park at Caneel Bay Resort and from the parking either walk a trail to Honeymoon Beach or there is a golf cart shuttle ride for a small fee. The shuttle leaves from the Caneel Bay Gift Shop and goes to and from Honeymoon Beach.

Watersports equipment is available at the Honeymoon Hut including snorkel gear, lounge chairs, kayaks, stand up paddleboards, floats and lockers. These can be rented individually as you like; or rent them all with a Day Pass.

The Honeymoon Beach Hut offers drinks, snacks and restrooms; and just next door Canella's Beach Bar sells freshly made sandwich wraps, homemade gelato ice cream, cold beer, wine, piña coladas and famous rum painkillers.

Honeymoon Beach All-Inclusive Watersports Daypass

Visit: viecotours.com

Contact or Call (877) 845-2925 (340) 779-2155

Experience St John's most romantic beach with the

All-Inclusive Day Pass; includes snorkel gear, life jacket, lounge chair, float, kayak, standup paddle board & locker. Relax in a hammock! Snorkel with sea turtles! Honeymoon Hut sells drinks & souvenirs with food available. Taxi to Caneel Bay Resort; then walk 8 minutes to Honeymoon Beach, or take a $5pp each way shuttle between the Caneel Bay parking and Honeymoon Beach. Another option, hike from Cruz Bay via Lind Point Trail to Honeymoon Beach. Perfect for wedding, corporate & private groups. $49 per adult. $10 per child. Book online using promo code VINOW for 10% discount or call toll free.

6.Salt Pond Bay

Salt Pond Bay is a beautiful bay with amazingly clear water. The beach is often sparsely populated because it is a longer drive from Cruz Bay then most of the popular beaches, and requires a short 7-10 minute hike downhill once at the parking lot. You can continue hiking around a nearby salt pond toward the ocean on the Drunk Bay Trail. A longish swim to the middle of the bay to a set of jagged rocks that break the surface offers good snorkeling. Snorkeling can also be enjoyed along the rocky sides of the bay, in particular the eastern coastline. The beach doesn't offer shade as foliage consists of short shrubs.

7.Francis Bay

Visit Francis Bay and you will find yourself on one of St. John's longest beaches. This beautiful beach has calm waters and a lovely, sandy shore. Often sparsely populated on weekdays its easy to find a nice quiet spot. Picnic tables are available. The Francis Bay Trail runs along a salt pond and offers great bird watching. There is good snorkeling for beginners along the western end of the beach towards Maho Bay. For strong swimmers, enter the water from the rocky section of other end of the beach. Halfway out from the bay's point begins a varied, narrow reef. For those with a kayak, Whistling Cay, adjacent to the bay, offers very good snorkeling.

Fins, a mask and a snorkel

Some of the popular beaches have watersports booths that rent snorkel gear. You can also rent gear for a few days from a dive shop. A popular question by visitors is "Should I buy or rent a set". Frequent visitors agree that you should buy a set. Here's why. To enjoy snorkeling your gear needs to fit you well, particularly your mask. A leaky mask can ruin a snorkeling experience. When buying your mask test it out by holding it to your face without the strap behind your head and inhale slightly through your nose. Let go of the mask, it should say in place; this indicates a good seal. Your fins should fit you snugly when dry because when you get in the ocean the water acts as a lubricant. Snorkels are easier because they are mostly one size fits all. If you get a bag for your gear make sure its a mesh type bag so that water and sand can drain out. An underwater camera is a great accessory; you can pick up a disposable underwater camera at your local supermarket. Another neat accessory is a Fish ID Card; a small, waterproof card that includes popular marine animals you might see while snorkeling.

Snuba

For those of you who like snorkeling and are not divers there is a middle ground option called super snorkeling! There are several types of super snorkeling, however only Snuba is available on St. John.

Snuba enables people with the use of a mask and breathing tube attached to a tank of air floating on the surface to explore shallow coral reefs and marine environments while swimming under the water.

Available to anyone from eight years old and up and doesn't require experience.

St. John offers rest, relaxation and an adequate amount of sporting activities. Plan the activities you would like to do most and have a great vacation!

Tip: Don't snorkel alone. Don't touch or stand on coral, it is very fragile. Don't feed the marine life non-fish food. Cereal, cake, bread, nuts, dog biscuits, leftover hotdogs from lunch are not part of marine creature's natural diets and are considered unhealthy for them. Do wear sunscreen on your back or wear a t-shirt. You can easily spend 30 minutes to an hour floating along admiring the fish and that is plenty of time for the bright tropical sunshine to leave you with a painful sunburn.

St. John: Watersports

The Virgin Islands has a huge playground all around its islands; the ocean! Our beautiful ocean and beaches combined with gorgeous year-round summer weather make Watersports hugely popular for residents and visitors. Whether you are looking for a bit of high in the sky fun with parasailing or a bit of speed with waverunners, you'll find them on St. John. If you have a sense of adventure, want to explore some of the coastline or beach hop you can look into renting a dinghy.

St. John Beaches

The Beautiful Beaches of St. John

It's no real wonder that the Virgin Islands were a favorite hangout of pirates, buccaneers, and privateers (ever a fluid distinction). With their numerous nooks and crannies to park a ship to ride out a storm or lay in waiting for ships passing along the many trade routes, they provided the ideal natural environment for an occupation predicated on quick, surprise raids. There's a good, nearby harbor for any wind and swell direction, and, especially useful to pirates, most of the harbors are sheltered on the land sides by mountains and hills. And the islands had another major attraction to pirate-folk: that elixir of the New World, rum. Invented in the Caribbean as a way to create a profit from the molasses that amounted to essentially industrial waste from sugar production, rum was cheap and easier to store on board than potable water.

These nooks and crannies, along with the reefs that are so treacherous to boating then and now, also have a pleasant side-effect for the less piratically inclined they create some of the world's most scenic beaches. The area's coral reefs create white sandy crescent beaches, and the many angles of headlands and rocky outcrops provide protection for pristine beaches. Water temperature (and air temperature, for that matter) doesn't vary much year around and sits around 79 to

83 degrees Fahrenheit (26 to 28 degrees Celsius). When you visualize an idyllic Caribbean sandy beach framed by beautiful turquoise seas, there's a good chance it's going to look quite a lot like one of St. John's picture perfect beaches. Not even those other inhabitants of humid, tropical climates mosquitoes and sand midges can spoil from the idyllic surroundings.

The view of Trunk Bay, in particular, from a nearby overlook, has become one of the most widely dispersed tropical beach views in the world, even if it's rarely identified as such. Caneel Bay, with its famous resort, and Hawk's Nest, with its palm trees and white sands, are precisely what you think of when you think of a Caribbean beach. And thanks to them being in a National Park, they're not overrun with people and overly commercialized.

Trunk Bay

The most famous and most visited of St. John's beaches, it looks like it was created for postcards, and there's a good chance you'll recognize the view from the nearby overlook from all manner of island getaway graphics and posters. A small rocky island on the northern end adds protection from ocean swells and in its submerged shadow is where the best of the beach's snorkeling can be found. With its underwater snorkeling trail really just some concrete signposts under the water with basic information about the marine life in situ its lifeguard station, change rooms, and snorkeling gear rental counter, it's probably one of the easiest to start at, especially with kids. There's a modest admission charge.

Cinnamon Bay

One of the longest beaches, Cinnamon Bay is also one of the most exposed, so if the winds and waves are coming from the north, it's not always the best option for swimming or snorkeling. But most of the time,

Cinnamon Bay is stunning. It's possible to "camp" at Cinnamon Bay in concrete bunker-like structures, and there's a newly renovated store onsite. But if you plan on camping there, I'd strongly recommend doing some research in online reviews ahead of time—it's not, as they say, everyone's cup of tea, and Maho Bay might be a better bet.

Maho Bay

One of the furthest beaches on the northern shore from Caneel Bay, it's yet another stunning beach. Next to the beach is an eco-resort.

Hawksnest Beach

The closest of the beaches to Cruz Bay with road access is also one of the prettiest. A small crescent of white sand lined with waving palm trees, it's just as you'd picture a Caribbean Beach should be.

Caneel Bay

With access jealously guarded by the eponymous resort, Caneel Bay has long been the hideout for the well-heeled set. The beach indeed, the entire peninsular is private property and open only to guests of the resort or patrons of the resort's restaurant. If you're looking for a luxury beach-side resort, Caneel Bay is a good bet.

Getting to the Beaches
Once you're on St. John, getting to the beaches is easy. St. John's taxis really more like open-back shuttle buses than conventional taxis run regularly from Cruz Bay along the main road and will pick up passengers anywhere along it. It's possible to rent a car and drive yourself, but cars can be short supply, are expensive, and you'll be dealing with roads best left to locals, not to mention driving on the wrong side of the road or the car (on St. John, the vehicles are left-hand drive but one drives on the left-hand side of the road). A more fun option, for those with boating inclinations, is to

rent a dinghy or power boat from Cruz Bay and approach by sea. Because it's a marine national park, beaching the boats on the sand is heavily frowned upon and most of the beaches are protected by no-boat zones, but several of the beaches offer mooring buoys just offshore, from whence it's a short swim ashore.

Denis Bay

Denis Bay is a pretty and quiet beach. Its powdery white sand shore is often sparsely populated, primarily because its only accessible by a rugged trail or by boat. The trail begins at the Peace Hill trail and descends to the western extreme of the bay.. Denis Bay is part of the National Park. There is fair to good snorkeling to be had. Bring snacks and drinks with you as there are no amenities. The property behind the tree line at the beach is private.

Nightlife

St. John Nightlife & Entertainment Guide

St. John is a small island with a very small island feel. The population is small, welcoming and friendly. St. Johnians like to 'hang out', have a drink, exchange stories and listen to music. If 'chilling out' is your type of ambiance than you will enjoy the small bars and open air 'watering holes' of St. John.

The nightlife on St. John tends to be more low-key then its sister island St. Thomas. Outings are a friendly affair. There are several bars around the island. Many focus on music, food and good times. Live music, including reggae bands, is a popular entertainment. Some very colorful bars can be found in Coral Bay. Cruz Bay is also home to several entertaining spots. It is not unusual in Cruz Bay to find people gathered in front of a small bar, sitting almost on the road drinking, talking and having a great time.

For a quieter more romantic night out on St. John have a nice dinner, desert and drinks at a great restaurant. There are several to choose from.

If you are staying at one of St. John's resorts you will find that there are several bars, lounges and restaurants at the resort; and that these places offer evening entertainment and an opportunity to mingle with locals and other visitors.

St. John from time to time has live performances including plays and concerts. During special holidays like Christmas and Carnival there are often great events to attend. Visit the Events Schedule for more information.

Shopping

Shopping on St. John, Virgin Islands
Shopping on St. John is unique and fun. Casual and entertaining shopping areas are in Cruz Bay and Coral

Bay. These two areas are the primary "towns" if anywhere on St. John can really be considered such. Quaint tropical buildings and gorgeous stone Caribbean structures house small stores that sell an assortment of items. Shops and boutiques on St. John are well known for unique items like handmade jewelry, local crafts, paintings and pottery.

VItraders.com

Visit: www.vitraders.com

Contact or Call (340) 774-1181

You can shop online for your favorite souvenirs, travel guides and maps from the Virgin Islands. VItraders.com has been serving customers for over 14 years. Planning a vacation and need a guide book, beach guide, map or bird watching book? VItraders.com has a great book section. Are you looking for souvenirs like wall calendars, cook books, Caribbean dolls, coloring books, hot sauce, magnets, postcards, mugs, Christmas Cards and ornaments, hats or shot glasses? You will find a nice selection of all of those and more. Click over to VItraders.com for Virgin Islands Books and Souvenirs.

In Cruz Bay, the main "town" and shopping area, you will find shops at Mongoose Junction, along King Street and at Wharfside Village – all are in walking distance from the ferry dock. A casual walk through Cruz Bay and you will find swim wear, bags, liquor, jewelry, art work and more – all in a delightfully calm and casual environment.

Mongoose Junction attracts the eye; it's a beautiful piece of art in itself and it houses many fantastic stores with fascinating items; handmade pottery, paintings, jewelry and even hand painted clothing! Get great deals on beautiful gold earrings and necklaces and pick up unique souvenirs.

Shopping Hours on St. John
Mongoose Junction

Normal hours: 10 am to 5 pm 7 days a week. A few stores open earlier (9 am) or close later (8 pm). During slow season and on weekends some shops close.

Cruz Bay is a small area so restaurants and bars are all in the same vicinity as the shops; making a break for lunch or a drink easy.

Shops in Coral Bay offer an assortment of t-shirts and souvenirs. Great restaurants are mixed in with the shops making shopping, having lunch and beach time a great and easy way to spend the day.

Resorts on St. John also offer shopping. Boutiques on hotel grounds offer an assortment of books, sundries, handicrafts, sportswear, sunglasses, watches and souvenirs.

Shopping on St. John is great fun; shops are individualized and unique. Walking through shady alleys, having a break on a beach front veranda or cool courtyard and purchasing special gifts is what it's all about. Happy Shopping!

Transportation

St. John Island Guide: Transportation

St. John's beauty is in the island; in its beaches, forests and historical ruins, and they are best explored by motored transportation. There are many trails within the National Park, therefore hiking during the day is a good option for getting around the park. Roads are narrow and without sidewalks in most cases so walking on roads should be done with great caution. St. John is hitch-hiking friendly.

Car Rental Information and Agencies

Renting a car will allow you the freedom to see the island, beach hop, visit different restaurants and thoroughly enjoy your time on St. John. Most rental agencies are located in Cruz Bay and there are several to choose from.

Inter-Island Ferry and Air Service

Inter-island travel is facilitated by ferry service between St. Thomas and St. John and commuter airlines on St. Thomas..

Scooters, Motorcycles, Bicycles

There are a few shops that rent scooters in Cruz Bay. Motorcycle rentals are not available. Bicycles are available for sport to ride on trails and are not used for transportation due to the steep, narrow nature of roads on St. John.

Taxis & Rates

Taxi Service is abundant on St. John. Popular spots like the ferry dock in Cruz Bay, Trunk Bay and Cinnamon Bay always have taxis waiting to assist you. Taxis can be called to pick you up at other destinations. Taxis charge per person and per destination, there are no metered taxis.

Public Transportation

The Vitran Bus System services various areas of the island. Vitran buses run along Centerline Road. The buses travel from the Cruz Bay ferry dock, through to Coral Bay and then to Salt Pond Bay. From Cruz Bay the bus leaves at 6am, 7am, and then 25 minutes pass the hour until 7:25pm. From Salt Pond Bay the bus leaves at 5am, 6am, 7am, 8am and then 10 minutes after the hour until 8:10pm. The fare is $1 a person. Senior Citizens receive a discounted fare of $.55. The Public Bus system is not very reliable, if you are on a tight or limited time schedule it is not a good idea to depend on the bus.

St. John: Car Rentals

St. John is a small island with many beaches and areas of interest. If you would like to explore the island at your leisure the best way to do it is by having your own mode of transportation. Many rental agencies are conveniently located in Cruz Bay, within walking distance of the ferry dock. Some agencies also have offices at the larger hotels.

Average prices on rentals range from $65 to $100 a day and differ depending on time of year or season. A Jeep Wrangler will run around $70 to $80. Larger vehicles go for $80 to $100. The latter price being for a 7 passenger minivan. Special packages and discounts are available. Be sure to book early during high season!

L & L Jeep Rental

Visit: www.bookajeep.com

Contact or Call (340) 776-1120 (340) 774-3975

L & L Jeep Rental welcomes you to St. John. We hope you have a pleasant stay here on our beautiful island.

For your convenience, we recommend renting a vehicle during your visit. Our fleet includes automatic, four wheel drive Jeep Wranglers (accommodates 1-4 passengers) and Jeep Liberties (accommodates 1-5 passengers), perfect for navigating our mountainous little island. Express check in and check out, an after hours emergency line and relationships with many villa companies and resorts are just some of the reasons L & L Jeep Rental is the right choice! Contact us to Book a Jeep!

Driving on St. John

➢ Driving in the Virgin Islands is on the left side of the road.

➢ Vehicles are typical American cars with left side steering.

➢ U.S. driver's licenses are valid for up to 90 days. Driver's holding international licenses must purchase a temporary foreign driver's permit.

These can be purchased from the Virgin Islands Bureau of Motor Vehicles. Since doing this can be difficult for visitor's they are available from car rental agencies who are allowed to pre-purchase them and have on hand to sell to visitor's renting vehicles. They are usually $25.

Should I rent a car or use taxis?

The question of whether to rely on taxis or rent a car is a frequently asked one. Below are a few of the answers:

➢ "You really should get a jeep if you want to see the island in its entirety, The roads are just awesome. I saw places I am sure the average person visiting did not."

➢ "We rent a vehicle on St. John. You could probably do fine without a vehicle staying at Cinnamon Bay just using taxis to get around. You might want to rent a vehicle for a couple of days to get around the island a bit more. If you're not going in peak season you can probably find a vehicle to rent just walking up to a few places in Cruz Bay in the morning. We wouldn't get anything but 4WD. Most of the time you won't need it, but if you need it and don't have it, there's no substitute. Roads are steep and windy. When they're wet, they can be very tough."

➤ "I highly recommend you rent a car. On the other hand, I guess it really depends on how much you are going to want to get out and explore. The farther the distance your villa is from Cruz Bay, the less you'll be able to rely on taxis. Cost wise, if you think you're going to make 3 or more trips a day away from the villa, it'll be cheaper to rent a car. Two trips a day and you'll probably break close to even."

➤ "The roads are safe on St. John. Comfort level at driving on them depends on the driver. The roads are steep in some areas, narrow in others, pretty much all paved, street signs exist, limited parking in Cruz Bay, pretty good parking at beaches and attractions. It takes a little bit to adjust to driving differently then you are used to but after a few hours you should be fine."

➤ "St John roads are steep and winding but most people respect that and drive accordingly. Just watch out for the big dump trucks and cement trucks and give them all the room you can. Go slow, enjoy the views and you should have no problem and be able to enjoy the stories you can tell when you get back home."

➤ "We always rent a car. We don't like being tied down to any one place."

➤ "I rented a Mitsubishi eclipse, a small, not much ground clearance, car. It presented no problem on St. John. After driving on St. John I can see that if the weather did not cooperate and the island got rain when you were there a jeep may come in handy as the hills are very steep and crooked. The roads get slick, I'm sure. Also, if you were going to take some roads less traveled that may be dirt or rocky a jeep may come in handy. Another note about our car experience when parking on the side of the road to go beach hopping some of the parking areas were nothing more than a worn out place into the trees. The drop off from the road was more than a few inches and our little car found it tough to get in out without scraping. I may also add that a car with a locking trunk was nice in that you could place anything of value inside and not have to worry about anything being gone when you got back."

➢ "If you drive slowly and enjoy the view it is not white knuckle. Roads have steep sections and sharp curves, but the drop offs aren't that bad. Rent the car so you can see all the fantastic beaches. Biggest problem will be finding parking in Cruz Bay."

➢ "St. John is curvy and hilly – kind of a roller coaster ride. I'm a little afraid of heights, but I had no problems. Most of the roads are well paved and in good shape. On the drive from Cruz Bay to Coral Bay on the Centerline Road I got sick and tired of putting the foot on the gas, move to the brake to slow for the corner, turn, go 75 feet and repeat the entire process. My leg was tired. No exaggeration, there must be a thousand curves between Cruz Bay and Coral Bay. But don't let the fact that the island is not suited to building straight highways deter you. It's the most beautiful driving in the world."

St. John: Taxis & Rates

Taxis are a popular transportation choice for visitors to St. John. The most popular taxi vehicle used is the open air safari (converted trucks; truck beds are customized with bench seating in an open-air covered area). Taxis on St. John are not metered; rates are per person and per destination and are set by the VI Taxicab Division. Taxi Rate Sheets are provided below.

Taxi Tips

➢ Taxis are almost always available at the ferry dock in Cruz Bay (during regular ferry schedule hours) and also at hotels. They frequently wait for passengers at the taxi stand area at Trunk Bay and Cinnamon Bay.

➢ Licensed taxi vehicles are labeled with: a taxi placard or dome light on the roof, license plates that indicate Taxi status, On Duty/Off Duty sign in the window of the vehicle and a sign, usually on the fender, indicating passenger capacity. The drivers personal identification/taxi license should be on the vehicles dash board.

➤ Although rates are standardized it is recommended that you speak to the driver and agree to your total rate (for you, your group, your luggage, waiting, tour) before boarding the taxi.

➤ Many taxis are multi-destination and some can carry up to 26 passengers; drivers will often wait to fill their vehicle before departing (particularly from the ferry dock and popular beach locations like Trunk Bay and Cinnamon Bay).

➤ See the Special Provisions Section after the rate sheets for sightseeing tour rates, luggage rates, private taxi rates, weekly rates and other information.

Taxi Rates

CRUZ BAY TO/FROM:	1 PERSON	2+ / EACH
Adrian Housing	7.00	6.00
Annaberg	13.00	9.00

Bethany Moravian Church	6.00	5.00
Bordeaux Mountain	17.00	11.00
Beth Cruz	6.00	5.00
Caneel Bay Plantation	6.00	5.00
Catherineburg	9.00	7.00
Chateau de Bordeaux	9.00	8.00
Chocolate Hole	7.00	6.00
Cinnamon Bay	9.00	7.00
Contant	6.00	5.00
Coral Bay	16.00	9.00
Dennis Bay	8.00	6.00
Desoto Bock House (East End)	25.00	15.00
Fish Bay	13.00	8.00
Francis Bay	13.00	9.00
Frank Bay	5.00	4.00
Gallows Point	5.00	4.00

St. John Island, USVI

Gill Hill	8.00	6.00
Maho Bay Beach	11.00	7.00
Golf Course	7.00	5.00
Great Cruz Bay	6.00	5.00
Grunwald	6.00	5.00
Hawksnest	6.00	5.00
Hurricane Hole	19.00	13.00
John's Head	9.00	7.00
Jumbie Beach	8.00	6.00
Lameshur	25.00	15.00
Leinster Bay	13.00	9.00
Maho Bay Campground	13.00	9.00
Mandahl	20.00	14.00
Pine Peace	5.00	4.00
Rendezous Bay (Cline Bay)	8.00	6.00
Reef Bay Trail	9.00	7.00

Paul Gibson

Salt Pond	20.00	14.00
Sunset Ridge	8.00	6.00
Susannaberg	8.00	6.00
Trunk Bay	8.00	6.00
Vie's (East End)	25.00	15.00
Westin	6.00	5.00
Zootenvaal	18.00	12.00
CORAL BAY TO/FROM:	1 PERSON	2+ / EACH
Adrian Housing	9.00	7.00
Annaberg	8.00	6.00
Blomingdale	6.00	5.00
Calabash Boom	6.00	5.00
Caneel Bay (via Northshore)	13.00	9.00
Cinnamon Bay	9.00	6.00
Desoto Bock House (East End)	9.00	6.00
Hurricane Hole	7.00	5.00

John's Folly School	6.00	5.00
Lamishur	9.00	6.00
Little Maho Bay	9.00	6.00
Mandahl	7.00	5.00
Salt Pond	7.00	6.00
Public Works	10.00	7.00
Susannaberg	10.00	7.00
Trunk Bay (via Centerline)	19.00	13.00
Trunk Bay (via North Shore)	9:00	6.00
Vie's (East End)	8.00	7.00
Zootenvaal	6.00	5.00
GALLOWS POINT TO/FROM:	1 PERSON	2+ / EACH
Annaberg	13.00	9.00
Caneel Bay	7.00	5.00
Cinnamon Bay	10.00	7.00
Maho Bay Beach	11.00	8.00

	1 PERSON	2+ / EACH
Golf Course	7.00	5.00
Hawksnest	7.00	5.00
Maho Bay Campground	13.00	9.00
Trunk Bay	8.00	6.00
CANEEL BAY TO/FROM:	1 PERSON	2+ / EACH
Chateau Bordeaux	12.00	10.00
Cinnamon Bay	8.00	6.00
Coral Bay (Via Centerline)	18.00	10.00
Gallows Point	7.00	5.00
Maho Bay Beach	10.00	7.00
Golf Course	8.00	6.00
Maho Bay Campground	12.00	8.00
Trunk Bay	7:00	5.00
Westin	8.00	6.00
WESTIN RESORT TO/FROM:	1 PERSON	2+ / EACH
Annaberg	15.00	11.00

St. John Island, USVI

Asolare	7.00	5.00
Chateau Bordeaux	12.00	10.00
Cinnamon Bay	11.00	9.00
Coral Bay	15.00	11.00
Dennis Bay	10.00	8.00
East End	27.00	18.00
Maho Bay Beach	12.00	9.00
Golf Course	7.00	5.00
Hawknest	8.00	7.00
Maho Bay Campground	15.00	11.00
Salt Pond	27.00	18.00
Susannaberg Clinic	10.00	8.00
Trunk Bay	10.00	8.00
Chateau Bordeaux To/From:	1 PERSON	2+ / EACH
Trunk Bay	8.00	7.00
Cinnamon Bay	7.00	6.00

Special Provisions for Taxi Operators

➢ The charges to areas not listed in the above schedule shall be arrived at by using the nearest tariffed place crossed to the next tariffed place ahead, based on one nearest to the passenger's destination.

➢ Taxi operators with On-duty sign on shall not refuse a passenger, unless the passenger is intoxicated and disorderly or in possession of a pet or animal (other than a seeing eye dog) that is not properly secured in a kennel case or other suitable container. There shall be no extra charge for seeing-eye dogs.

➢ Kennel Charges: Large Kennel – $30, Small Kennel – $20.

➢ Round trip fares: double the one-way fare plus waiting charges.

➢ Waiting charges: $1.00 per minute. First five minutes free.

➢ Radio/Phone Call: One person, the fare plus one third of the basic fare. More than one person; add $1.00 to each passenger.

➢ Between midnight and 6:00am, there shall be an additional charge of $2.00 per person.

➢ Any person requesting a taxi exclusively for themselves: rate to be negotiated between the taxi operator and passenger(s).

➢ Luggage: A flat rate of $2 per bag shall be added to the fare for each passenger. The rate for items greater than 30"x20" shall not exceed $4 per item.

➢ Hourly Rates (1-4 passengers): Sedan/Mini Van $40; Van/Safari(14 pax capacity) $55; Safari $80. Rates for additional passengers will be negotiated between the taxi operator and passenger(s).

➤ All passengers must be discharged at their precise requested locations when fare is accepted and agreed to.

➤ Sightseeing Tours: 2 hours – One passenger $50; two or more passengers $25 per person. 3 hours – One passenger $70; two or more passengers $35 per person.

Accommodations

Accommodations on St. John, Virgin Islands

St. John provides relative seclusion for vacationers. There is a mix of resorts, camping, inns and villas to choose from; they fill up quickly, particularly during winter months.

The main "towns" are Cruz Bay and Coral Bay. Several small inns are available in those areas, as are a few vacation homes and condos. A stay in these areas will allow easy access to popular restaurants, bars and shopping. Access to beaches will require a short 8-20 minute drive depending on destination.

A popular choice for visitors to St. John is a villa. You will feel like a king or queen in one of these spectacular homes. Private pools, guest services including caterer if wanted, amazing views and tranquility will make you want to stay forever. Villas are located throughout the island.

On St. John you will find a few luxury resorts, they invite you to be waited on; to dine on beachfront property and to have your every reasonable request met. Situated on spectacular beaches, offering luxury and fabulous diversions the resorts on St. John are a perfect retreat.

Featured Accommodations

Island Getaways, Inc.

Visit: www.islandgetawaysinc.com

Contact or Call (888) 693-7676 (340) 693-7676

Island Getaways Inc. offers you a wonderful selection of 2 to 6 bedroom villas. All vacation rentals are fully furnished and reflect the open air tropical feeling of the island. Tell us what you are looking for and we will suggest villas that suit your needs. Each villa is equipped with a modern kitchen containing essential appliances. All linens, paper products, beach chairs, towels and coolers are provided. Island Getaways is your best source for luxury villa rentals on St. John. Call or email us today!

Coral Bay's Windspree Vacation Homes

Visit: www.windspree.com

Contact or Call (888) 742-0357 (340) 693-5423

Windspree Vacation Homes in peaceful Coral Bay, St John offers an alternative to hotels and resorts. Live the dream vacation in a well appointed home with breathtaking views of the Caribbean Sea by day and the starlit skies at night. Enjoy cool tropical breezes year round as you lounge in the privacy of your own pool or spa or spend your days hiking, snorkeling, exploring ruins, boating and more. Windspree Vacation Homes provides an affordable selection of villas and homes for every budget. Visit our website for more information and to view our great selection of vacation rentals!

The Westin St. John Resort Villas

Visit: www.starwoodhotels.com

Call (866) 716-8108

Overlooking Great Cruz Bay, The Westin St. John Resort Villas is a 47-acre paradise, offering a number of resort amenities and intuitive services all framed by picture-perfect Caribbean ocean views. Your stylish sanctuary is a spacious one-, two- or even three-bedroom villa or townhouse of up to 2,850 square feet that comfortably accommodates up to eight adults. Each villa includes fully equipped kitchens, a washer and dryer, private balconies with ocean views, and whirlpool tubs. Explore our website to discover all that The Westin St. John Resort Villas has to offer for your next memorable vacation.

Sea Shore Allure

Visit: www.seashoreallure.com

Contact or Call (855) 779-2800 (340) 779-2800

Discover modern amenities at Sea Shore Allure. Our exclusive St. John resort features eight boutique condominiums that overlook the stunning waters of the US Virgin Islands. Nestled in a quiet spot near downtown Cruz Bay, our resort's location, amenities, and accommodations are second to none. Whether you spend your days lounging at our Blue Havana pool, watching the sunset from the hot tub on our rooftop terrace, or touring the island - Sea Shore Allure is an exclusive resort that lets you enjoy a quiet vacation that is still close to all of the best shopping and dining on St. John. Rated #1 on TripAdvisor for Hotels on St. John.

St. John Vacation Ownership & Rentals

Visit: www.vacationownership.com

Contact or Call (866) 633-1030

Vacation ownership properties, or timeshares, on the island of St. John offer a unique accommodation experience unlike any other. Located within 5 star resorts, guests will indulge in luxuries like modern bathrooms with premium toiletries, multiple airy bedrooms, private balconies with panoramic vistas, and plush king-sized beds. On-site you'll discover a wealth of things to do: cocktail lounges, sparkling infinity pools, lively entertainment, and restaurants can all be found at these spectacular resorts. By renting or buying a St. John timeshare through VacationOwnership.com, you'll have the opportunity to save hundreds off resort costs while not having to sacrifice any of the aforementioned luxuries.

Catered to Vacation Homes

Visit: www.cateredto.com

Contact or Call (800) 424-6641 (340) 776-6641

At Catered To Vacation Homes we offer a bit of paradise for every taste from moderate to luxurious. Our private homes are beautifully furnished and landscaped, all with spectacular deck views and most with swimming pools or spas. Features include fully equipped kitchens, all linens, TV's, DVD, CD and IPod ready stereos, internet access, gas grills, beach chairs, beach towels and coolers. Join us and be... Catered To! Visit us on-line or call us for more information!

Calabash Cottages

Visit: www.calabashcottages.com

Contact or Call (340) 776-6368

Calabash Cottages in Coral Bay offers a range of

secluded and romantic one bedroom cottages and villas for couples. Larger groups can combine our homes. Our smallest cottage has a beautiful view, a private hot tub and is a great choice for couples traveling on a budget. Our largest offering is a spacious one bedroom villa with a pool and a hot tub. Each house is private, located in a very quiet area of the island and has a beautiful view as well as a spa. We can arrange for discounted car rentals. We also meet our guest upon arrival to escort them to their home away from home.

Carefree Get-Aways on St. John

Visit: www.carefreegetaways.com

Contact or Call (888) 643-6002 (340) 779-4070

We are a villa rental and management company located on St John. Carefree Getaways provides a delightful variety of accommodations on St John, from condos and cottages to Caribbean style rentals, ocean view vacation villas to waterfront luxury for honeymoon retreats to family fun! We can provide our guests with ideas for catering services, provisioning, private chefs, boat and snorkeling excursions, and assist in arranging rental cars. Please enjoy exploring our web site and we look forward to hearing from you!

Hillcrest Guest House

Visit: www.hillcreststjohn.com

Contact or Call (340) 776-6774 (340) 998-8388

The perfect place to feel human again. The peacefulness is rejuvenating, the breeze, the flowers and atmosphere. Located on a hillside where the gentle trade winds blow all night and day. The Front and Caribbean Ocean View Suites are ideal for couples and honeymooners. The Sunset, Orchid, Peaceful Retreat and Tropical Garden Suites are suitable for small families and small groups. Our hotel is conveniently located in a residential area just above

Cruz Bay, minutes from the beach and the National Park. Complimentary menu available. Visit our web site for more information.

Destination St. John

Visit: www.destinationstjohn.com

Contact or Call (800) 562-1901 (340) 779-4647

We'll help you find the perfect home to suit your want and needs, from a spirited family holiday home to a luxurious and romantic hideaway. We can even assist you with car rental and excursion reservations, or anything else you'll need on your St. John vacation. Visit our website to browse the selection of vacation homes we offer.

Caneel Bay Resort

Visit: www.CaneelBay.com

Contact or Call (855) 226-3358 (340) 776-6111

At Caneel Bay it's time to unwind in pristine natural surroundings and low-key luxury. The resort, nestled within the Virgin Islands National Park on St. John, boasts 166 charming accommodations. Seven secluded beaches border 170 lush Caribbean acres where Caneel's accommodations blend into the landscape. Relax as island breezes whisper through plantation shutters and our discerning staff attends to your every need. Perched atop the resort's 18th-century sugar mill ruins, ZoZo's at the Sugar Mill offers a menu of northern Italian fare presented by famed local restaurateur John Ferrigno and his team. Whether you are looking for a romantic Caribbean getaway, family vacation, or relaxing escape, Caneel Bay is the ideal destination to exceed your expectations.

Seaview Homes

Visit: www.seaviewhomes.com

Contact or Call (888) 625-2963 (340) 776-6805

Seaview Homes offer 2 to 5 bedroom fully furnished villa accommodations and vacation homes with all amenities; including some with pools, hot tubs and air conditioning. Our homes and villas all have commanding ocean views and are close to the famous North Shore beaches in the National Park. On island property managers can assist with boat charters, island tours, jeep rentals, fishing and diving. We can coordinate catering and chef services as well. Let us help you plan a Caribbean vacation of a lifetime.

Vacation Vistas

Visit: www.vacationvistas.com

Contact or Call (888) 334-5222 (340) 776-6462

Vacation Vistas has been providing excellence in vacation villa rentals and property management on the island of St. John for over 24 years. We offer a wide range of island style affordable homes to luxury private villas for weekly rentals. Visit our website to browse our selection of villas, amenities and availability. Call us today to reserve your rental or check our specials and last minute discounts.

In contrast to the main developed areas the remainder of the St. John, primarily the National Park areas remain forested and undisturbed. St. John boasts some of the most beautiful beaches and dramatic vistas to be seen in the Virgin Islands. To enjoy the National Park a stay at a campground will meet all your needs.

Other Accommodations

NAME	TYPE	PHONE
Cinnamon Bay Campground	Campground	(340) 776-6330
Concordia Campground	Campground	(340) 693-5855
St. John Inn	Inn	(340) 693-8688
The Inn at Tamarind Court	Inn	(340) 776-6738

Real Estate

Real Estate on St. John, Virgin Islands

St. John is unique; it offers the opportunity to own a dream home with magnificent ocean view on an island that is two-thirds protected from development by the National Park Service. Price tags fitting of a dream home nestled on a beautiful, protected Caribbean island are of course attached! The allure of St. John is in the lush green hills and beautiful white sand beaches. The island offers a slow pace of living and is home to a small community of about 4,200 people.

There are currently (September 2016) 161 houses on the market, ranging in size from a 554 square foot cottage on a .539-acre lot in Carolina; to a 3 bedroom, 3.5 bath luxury 6,596 square foot house on 1.1 acres in prestigious Peter Bay Estate. Most houses are designed with open styled floor plans, high ceilings and large decks to take advantage of the trade winds and the wonderful views. There are 63 houses listed below 1 million dollars. There are 98 houses listed that are over 1 million dollars.

House Sales

YEAR	TOTAL HOUSES SOLD	LOW	HIGH	AVERAGE
2000	41	$120,000	3.8 Million	$633,768
2001	46	$130,000	1.8 Million	$594,294
2002	57	$75,000	5 Million	$837,129
2003	61	$180,000	3.2 Million	$931,142
2004	43	$341,700	4.5 Million	$1,242,627
2005	54	$450,000	8.75 Million	$1,789,315
2006	33	$318,000	4.25 Million	$1,454,373
2007	29	$295,000	14 Million	$1,982,914
2008	23	$250,000	4.6 Million	$1,502,872
2009	22	$240,000	6.5 Million	$1,283,182
2010	20	$495,000	3 Million	$1,285,075
2011	27	$135,000	12 Million	$1,722,222

2012	28		$325,000	8.45 Million	$1,183,607
2013	48		$165,000	3.5 Million	$1,054,698
2014	40		$145,000	7.75 Million	$1,049,862
2015	38		$189,000	4 Million	$1,074,847

Most residents finance their homes through conventional mortgages with local banks. Interest rates are slightly higher in the Virgin Islands than on the mainland. A typical down payment is 20 to 30 percent. Banks require earthquake and windstorm insurance with mortgages; the cost is around 2-3% of replacement value.

Presently on the market there are 276 undeveloped land sites for sale ranging in price from $75,000 for .32-acre lot in Coral Bay; to 5.5 million for a 4.5 acre lot near Maho Bay Beach. Looking for a private island? Recently Thatch Cay, 237 acres, was on the market at $24,000,000. Properties within the National Park but not park owned are traditionally the most expensive. Land development and subdivision, like in Rendevous & Ditleff, have increased the availability of land lots within the last couple of years.

Factors to consider when looking for land include; location, view, access to the property and any site preparations that might be necessary in order to build. The average lot size is half an acre.

Land Lot Sales

YEAR	TOTAL LAND LOTS SOLD	LOW	HIGH	AVERAGE
2000	80	$23,250	$2.5 Million	$195,644
2001	96	$25,000	$1.1 Million	$168,093
2002	141	$34,500	$2.4 Million	$200,362
2003	167	$35000	$6 Million	$370,202
2004	106	$85,000	$8 Million	$530,141

2005	68	$110,000	$3.9 Million	$560,389
2006	49	$179,000	$1.4 Million	$496,144
2007	24	$92,500	$6,574,950	$726,519
2008	20	$115,000	$1.8 Million	$440,475
2009	19	$60,000	$3.5 Million	$380,553
2010	16	$75,000	$875,000	$248,125
2011	20	$72,000	$843,183	$287,865
2012	33	$55,000	$13.9 Million	$776,664
2013	31	$49,500	$2.5 Million	$396,016
2014	31	$65,500	$1.65 Million	$408,782
2015	44	$63,000	$970,000	$208,680

Building a home starts at around $350 per square foot and is affected largely by materials used for building and finishing. Keep in mind that preparations and special structural requirements may need to be met making the total cost of the construction project more. A cistern for water storage and a septic tank are necessary components of a home on St. John. The cistern alone will account for almost 10 percent of the total building cost. Land owners should depend on the experts when it comes to building on St. John; plans must be prepared by an architect, engineer or drafts-person licensed in the Virgin Islands.

There are 20 condo developments on St. John, some are small with just a few units while others are large. Most are located in or close to Cruz Bay. Currently on the market there are 24 condos.

Condo Sales

YEAR	TOTAL CONDOS SOLD	LOW	HIGH	AVERAGE

St. John Island, USVI

2000	15	$68,333	$320,000	$181,900
2001	16	$85,000	$335,000	$219,852
2002	14	$90,000	$350,000	$209,457
2003	7	$225,000	$460,000	$350,358
2004	13	$220,000	$925,000	$567,885
2005	12	$350,000	$990,000	$689,750
2006	6	$425,000	$1,035,000	$635,667
2007	6	$275,000	$1,250,000	$613,000
2008	15	$390,000	$789,000	$634,923
2009	6	$222,500	$1,200,000	$605,583
2010	7	$200,000	$932,300	$467,043
2011	5	$375,000	$550,000	$430,000
2012	9	$290,000	$850,000	$501,667
2013	8	$343,000	1 Million	$613,688
2014	9	$380,000	1.05 Million	$714,924
2015	12	$172,705	$748,250	$363,054

There are 170 time share units currently listed. The majority of which are located at Virgin Grand Estates & Villas and Westin Vacation Club, both in Chocolate Hole. Time shares range from $2,995 for a 1-week period in a 500 square foot studio on a beach front resort property; to $138,000 for a one-month period in a 3 bedrooms, 3 bath house.

There are presently 12 commercial opportunities available. They include a restaurant at $315,000; and a boat charter business at $189,000.

The overall inventory of St. John real estate at this time includes 643 listings.

Market Inventory Table, St. John

DATE	ALL	HOMES	LOTS	TIMESHARE	CONDOS	COMMERCIAL
August 2005	372	55	157	135	12	13
April 2006	549	101	249	122	50	27
February 2007	589	124	262	135	51	17

September 2008	702	117	258	238	58	30
October 2009	735	126	251	299	40	19
August 2010	708	137	262	248	46	15
August 2011	663	147	248	213	42	13
May 2012	689	166	269	198	44	12
August 2013	616	142	266	172	27	9
March 2015	672	165	294	178	27	8
September 2016	643	161	276	170	24	12

The National Park protects about two thirds of the St. John leaving limited amounts of property for development, this factor adds to both the desire of owning property and the high prices. Contact the featured real estate agents listed above for more information on property on St. John.

Getting Here

Getting to St. John (from St. Thomas)

Whether your vacation is on St. John or you are visiting St. Thomas and want to head over to St. John for the day – you will be taking a boat to travel between the two islands.

Things to Know

➢ St. John does not have an airport. Travelers must fly into the Cyril E. King Airport on St. Thomas (airport code: STT) and then continue to St. John by boat.

➢ You can travel between St. Thomas and St. John using a public ferry or a car barge; how to directions on taking both are available below. You can also travel between St. Thomas and St. John by private water taxi/boat..

➢ There are two ferry departure points on St. Thomas for the passenger ferry to St. John; one is in Charlotte Amalie and the other is in Red Hook.

➢ There is a ferry terminal in Charlotte Amalie that is used for ferries going to the British Virgin Islands. The ferry from Charlotte Amalie to St. John does not leave from that terminal.

➢ The car barge from St. Thomas to St. John departs only from Red Hook.

➢ Once in a while people confuse St. John (the island in the Virgin Islands) and St. John's (the capital city in Antigua). Antigua is a different Caribbean island, not part of the USVI, and it is 210 miles away from St. John. Mixing them up can be a pricey mistake if you have to change your flight or cancel hotel reservations. So remember the island in the USVI is St. John (no s).

How to take the Passenger Ferry

From St. Thomas to St. John

Step 1: Choose a ferry: Charlotte Amalie to St. John; or Red Hook to St. John. The Charlotte Amalie ferry is closer to the Airport (about 3 miles; 10 minute drive in low traffic); and also to the Cruise Ship Docks (about 1.5 miles; 7 minute drive in low traffic). The Charlotte Amalie schedule has 3 departures a day. There is no terminal, the ferry picks up right off the Charlotte Amalie waterfront. The Red Hook ferry is about 10 miles from the airport, about a 35 minute drive in low traffic, and about 8-9 miles from the Cruise Ship Docks. The Red Hook ferry has departures every hour on the hour from early morning to midnight. There is a ferry terminal in Red Hook with benches and a small bar. Reservations are not required for either ferry.

Step 2: Get to the ferry. So you've chosen which ferry you want to take; now you need to get there probably from the airport, cruise ship dock or your hotel. You should try to be at the ferry at least 15 minutes before departure. You can take a taxi, rent a car and drive yourself or try public transportation. If you are at the cruise ship dock and taking the Charlotte Amalie ferry, you could walk; it's about 1.5 miles and would take about 30-35 minutes. If you are driving yourself; there is a paid parking lot in Charlotte Amalie called Fort Christian Parking Lot – it's a short 2-3 minute walk from the ferry. And if driving to the passenger ferry in Red Hook there is a paid parking lot at the Red Hook Ferry Terminal. If it's full there are a couple paid parking lots on the hillsides across the street.

Step 3: Buy your tickets. For the Charlotte Amalie ferry you buy the tickets from the crew once the ferry arrives. For the Red Hook ferry you buy the ticket at the terminal. You can purchase a one way ticket, or round trip. There is a surcharge for luggage. Credit cards are not accepted; cash only.

Step 4: Board the ferry. Hand your ticket to the ferry attendant, get on the ferry and enjoy the ride. The ferry boats have enclosed seating on the main deck, and open air seating on the top deck. From Charlotte Amalie to St. John the ferry ride takes about 35 minutes. From Red Hook to St. John the ferry ride is about 15 minutes.

Step 5: Arrive in Cruz Bay, St. John. From there you can explore Cruz Bay on foot. Take a taxi to visit the island. There is a taxi stand at the end of the ferry dock. You can walk to a car rental company and rent a vehicle. If you are staying on St. John and your hotel or villa representative is meeting you – they will usually meet you near the end of the ferry dock.

From St. John to St. Thomas
Step 1: Select a departure time. Ferries depart from Cruz Bay Ferry Dock. to select the departure time that

works for you. Arrive at Ferry Dock at least 15 minutes prior to departure.

Step 2: Buy tickets. If you already have your ticket, proceed to the waiting area. If you need a ticket there is a ticket booth; specify whether you want a ticket for the Red Hook or Charlotte Amalie ferry. The waiting area is covered and gated; an attendant opens the gate when the ferry is ready for boarding.

Step 3: Board the ferry. Hand your ticket to the ferry attendant, get on the ferry and enjoy the ride. You may want to double check with the attendant collecting the ticket that you are boarding the correct ferry (to Red Hook or to Charlotte Amalie).

Step 4: Arrival in St. Thomas. If your destination is Red Hook and you need a taxi, there is a taxi stand at the Red Hook Ferry terminal. If your destination is Charlotte Amalie, there are typically taxis in the area.

How to take the Car Barge

From St. Thomas to St. John

Step 1: Choose a departure time. The car barges depart from Red Hook on St. Thomas to Enighed Pond, St. John. There are two companies that operate car barges..

Step 2: Drive to Red Hook. The car barge and passenger ferry terminal are right next to each other; each has its own entrance. Arrive about 25 minutes prior to departure time. There is a port tax of $3 per Car, small SUV, Motorcycle; $4 per truck, van, large SUV. The port tax is paid to an attendant in a booth just at the entry area for loading on the car barge.

Step 3: Waiting area. An attendant in the car barge loading area will typically ask what barge you plan to take; and instruct you on where to place your car. Wait in your car until the barge is ready to be loaded.

Step 4: Boarding the car barge. The barge attendants will direct driver's onto the car barge, and indicate where to park on the barge. You will reverse your vehicle onto the car barge.

Step 5: Buy tickets. Once on the barge, you can either stay in your car, or you can get out and sit on the upper deck. An attendant will approach you at your car, or on the deck, to sell you a ticket. You can purchase one way or round trip. No credit cards, cash only. A receipt will be provided; and the return ticket if you purchased a round trip fare. When purchasing your round trip ticket, double check that your return ticket can be used on the other barge service; and also check the return times. The return times are often listed on your ticket/receipt.

Step 6: Enjoy the ride over. If you are sitting on the deck, start heading back to your car once you get close to the dock area in St. John. The arrival place is Enighed Pond, just outside Cruz Bay.

From St. John to St. Thomas

Step 1: Choose a departure time. There is only one departure point for the car barge to St. Thomas, and that is Enighed Pond. There are two companies that operate car barges..

Step 2: Drive to Enighed Pond. There is an attendant outside the loading area that will ask you which car barge you intend to take; or if you already have a ticket they might ask to see the ticket so they can direct you to the correct car line for that barge.

Step 3: Boarding. Wait in car line until the attendant directs the line to start moving toward the barge. You will reverse your vehicle onto the car barge. The attendant will instruct you on where to park on the barge.

Step 4: Buy tickets. Once on the barge, you can either stay in your car, or you can get out and sit on the upper deck. An attendant will approach you at your car, or on the deck, to sell you a ticket or collect your existing ticket. You can purchase one way or round trip. No credit cards, cash only. A receipt will be provided; and the return ticket as well if you purchased a round trip fare. Be sure to ask if the return ticket can be used on another barge. Also confirm the return times – usually they are printed on the receipt.

Step 5: Enjoy the ride over. If you are sitting on the deck, start heading back to your car once you get close to the dock area in Red Hook, St. Thomas.

Restaurants

Dining St. John, Virgin Islands

Restaurants on St. John offer you various levels of enjoyable dining experiences. From casual outdoor dining to five course meals on patios over looking moonlit Cruz Bay, you will enjoy it all. Experienced chefs create mouth-watering entrees, often offering a large selection from continental cuisine to French, Italian and Caribbean foods.

Featured Dining

Mathayom Private Chefs ~ St. John Catering

Visit: www.stjohncatering.com

Contact or Call (877) 690-9393 (340) 777-5464 (340) 998-8670

Gourmet Drop-Off makes life a little easier by offering a large selection of fresh creations for dinner and breakfast. Whether you are just arriving or have had a long day on the water, it is one less thing to worry about. For a little more pampering consider a Private Chef. Formal or casual, our team will come to your location, set up your dining area, and serve you a one-of-a-kind menu. Each event has a unique bill of fare that has been customized for you. Visit our website to view past menus and get a feel of the food we produce. Allow yourself to truly relax while on vacation, contact us today!

In quaint Cruz Bay there are several narrow roads forming a small grid. Along these roads are several restaurants. There are a few restaurants right on the water. They offer pleasant ocean breezes and a great view. A short walk into Cruz Bay and you will find more restaurants offering everything from causal dining with BBQ chicken wings and beer to shrimp appetizers and steak dinners.

Cruz Bay is not the only area beckoning to your taste buds to enjoy its restaurants; you can also head out to Coral Bay for some causal and fun dining.

If you want a more formal dining experience the resorts on the islands have great restaurants that you can go to or there are several fabulous spots on the hillsides around Cruz Bay.

Other Dining

NAME	LOCATION	PHONE
Asolare	Caneel Hill	(340) 779-4747
Banana Deck	Cruz Bay	(340) 693-5055
Caneel Beach Terrace	Caneel Bay Resort	(340) 693-6111
Cafe Concordia	Salt Pond Bay	(340) 693-5855
Deli Grotto	Mongoose Junction	(340) 777-3061
Fish Trap	Cruz Bay	(340) 693-9994
High Tide Bar & Seafood Grill	Cruz Bay	(340) 714-6169
La Tapa	Cruz Bay	(340) 693-4199
Lime Inn	Cruz Bay	(340) 779-4199
Mango Deli	Westin Resort	(340) 693-8000
Morgan's Mango	Cruz Bay	(340) 693-8141
Skinny Legs	Coral Bay	(340) 779-4982

| Waterfront Beach Bistro | Cruz Bay | (340) 777-7755 |

Wedding Planning

Getting Married on St. John, Virgin Islands

Does your dream wedding take place on a secluded beach? How about at sunset with steel pan music playing? Or perhaps on a sailboat! Whatever your tropical dream wedding entails, it can be arranged on St. John. Ceremonies can be elaborate or simple. Perhaps you'd like to have your wedding at Annaberg Plantation, Hawksnest Beach or a gazebo overlooking the beach. St. John provides a truly amazing location for saying "I do". Spend your honeymoon on St. John in a private villa or be pampered at a resort.

Mathayom Private Chefs ~ St. John Catering

Visit: www.stjohncatering.com

Contact or Call (877) 690-9393 (340) 777-5464 (340)

998-8670

Whether your wedding or banquet is formal, casual, assisted, family style, cocktail, or buffet we will work with you to make your special function memorable for every guest. We can do Asian, Caribbean, Italian, Vegetarian or a menu theme based around your party. Our most common requests are for our Caribbean Beach BBQ and our Island Fancy Menu. Enjoy them as they are or alter them to suit your individual needs. Equipment rentals are also available for a smooth all-inclusive dining experience. For more information visit our website or contact us by phone or email.

Island Style Weddings

Visit: www.islandstyleweddings.com

Contact or Call (340) 774-1484

The Caribbean has captured your heart! Sugar white sand, tranquil breezes and turquoise waters are calling you. We are here to guide you, partner with you and to share all of our island expertise. We want to design the perfect Caribbean celebration that reflects your style and personality. Your Island Style Wedding is your first statement as a married couple. Let us help you make your vision a reality. This is your day and we would be honored to be a part of it.

Island Bliss Weddings

Visit: www.islandblissweddings.com

Contact or Call (340) 514-2685

One of the most innovative wedding planning services in the US Virgin Islands, Island Bliss Weddings has helped couples plan intimate ceremonies for those that wish to elope to elegant wedding weekends for those that want to celebrate with all their family & friends in our beautiful tropical islands. We understand it can be a little stressful to plan from so far away, it is our goal to make sure that our couples arrive without a worry in their heads! We take care of each detail and make sure your day is executed flawlessly, so you all you have to do is enjoy your time in the islands and begin your new lives together with a heart full of love and smiles.

Ceremonies of St. John

Visit: www.usviwedding.com

Contact or Call (888) 282-3933 (340) 693-7362

Congratulations on your engagement! We know you have a unique expression of your love and we are here to convey your vision. Say, "I Do", on a pristine white beach, in plantation ruins, at a luxury villa, on a private yacht, or in one of the oldest churches in the Caribbean. Our staff has years of experience in planning island weddings. Ceremonies of St John is the first wedding planning company located on St. John. Consider us your friend on St. John and allow us to design your special day.

Honeymoon Beach Weddings & Wedding Parties

Visit: viecotours.com

Contact or Call (877) 845-2925 (340) 779-2155

Honeymoon Beach is St John's premier beach destination your wedding party will never forget! Caneel Bay Resorts wedding planners coordinate with Virgin Islands Ecotours to arrange an unforgettable wedding bash with beach rental, ordained minister, tented bar, a kayak filled with ice and beer, live music, BBQ lunch, homemade gelato ice cream, beach attendants, hammocks, restrooms, gift shop, picnic tables, beach games, lots of shade and all day beach fun with lounge chairs, multi person party floats, kayaks, SUP and snorkel gear for everyone! Plan the best for your friends and family for groups up to 250! Call Virgin Island Ecotours for more information.

Wedding Consultants

A wedding consultant based in the Virgin Islands is your best resource for planning your wedding.

Whether the consultant is affiliated with a hotel or is in private business their knowledge of island weddings will make everything so much easier for you. Hotel packages might run anywhere from $550 up to $3000+. Prices depend on the package and can include the basics; a great location and the minister or can include bouquets, cake, photographer, champagne, limo, crystal flutes, videographer and live music.

Private consultants can arrange your wedding basically anywhere you choose but often will suggest the areas that are best suited for such an event. Packages can be basic to elaborate with prices around $300 and up. A consultant can take care of everything for you; processing the license, getting a great photographer, flowers, cake, caterers, transportation and if necessary even witnesses! They will insure that your day is extra special, just the way it should be!

The Virgin Islands are perfect for anniversaries and renewing vows! Consultants can plan these events as well and make it extra special for just the two of you or for the whole family. Contact a local wedding consultant and start planning your island dream wedding or vow renewal.

If you are planning to arrange the wedding yourself you will find wedding license information for the USVI below.

Request Marriage License Applications

The marriage license application fee is $200 ($100 for application fee and $100 for the license). There is an 8 day waiting and processing period, which can be waived depending on circumstances. The application is good for 1 year. Court marriages in front of a judge are performed on weekdays by appointment and will cost around $200. Religious ceremonies should be arranged directly with church officials. If either party has been divorced, a certified copy of the divorce decree must be presented. If you are requesting a marriage license through the mail, without the help of a local wedding consultant you will have to pick up the license yourself on arrival. This can only be done of regular business days.

St. Thomas /St. John

Superior Court of the Virgin Islands

P.O. Box 70

St. Thomas, USVI 00804

Telephone: (340)774-6680

Other Information

Personal Concierge

Travel Specialists & Personal Concierge on St. John

St. John has a lot to offer a visitor, and travel specialists that know the island well can help you plan the family vacation to remember, a perfect destination wedding or the corporate event that your employees talk about for years. They have researched the options that are available, worked with the service providers and can bring together all the parts to ensure your travel requests are met. Whether you are looking for a personal vacation concierge to help with lining up fun activities like a romantic sailing excursion or a team building scavenger hunt, getting a car rental, stocking your villa with groceries before you arrive... or banquet space, group transportation and meeting the needs of a big group; they can help.

Blue Sky Luxury Concierge

Visit: www.blueskyconcierge.com

Contact or Call (615) 604-2447

Blue Sky offers luxury concierge, provisioning and private event planning services for individuals, families and corporations visiting the Virgin Islands. Allow us to find the perfect rental villa or yacht for your vacation.

We can plan a variety of activities such as boat charters around the Virgin Islands, sunset sails, paddle board & kayak tours, in-villa massages & chefs, dive excursions, childcare, private transportation from the St. Thomas airport to St. John, rental cars, etc. Planning a corporate retreat, incentive trip or 50th birthday party? From small intimate parties to large-scale corporate events allow Blue Sky turn your vacation and event dreams into a reality

Groceries / Catering

St. John: Villa Provisioning & Catering

Staying in a villa or vacation home on St. John is a perfect way to enjoy your vacation. One of the benefits of vacation homes is that you have a full kitchen. You can have some of your meals in the comfort of your fabulous island home. Of course grocery shopping and cooking might not be the top thing to do on your vacation list; so have someone do it for you! Start your vacation right away by having your villa already stocked with all the things from your grocery list. Villa provisioning and grocery delivery is the way to go.

Another great option is hiring a personal chef to come over and prepare a wonderful meal for you. They can also prepare the meal and drop it off if you prefer. Having a wedding party and need a meal for a group, sure thing. Planning a corporate event and need catering, they can handle it. Get in touch, let them know what your grocery, dinner and catering needs are and let them put it all together for you.

Mathayom Private Chefs ~ St. John Catering

Visit: www.stjohncatering.com

Contact or Call (877) 690-9393 (340) 777-5464 (340) 998-8670

Your vacation time is valuable! Why clog up your itinerary with grocery shopping? We have all your basics, as well as liquor, beer and wine. Someone in your group love to grill? Let them enjoy the limelight with none of the prep work with prepped grill fare. Plan on staying in but don't want to cook? Choose from a large selection of fresh creations for dinner and breakfast with Gourmet Drop-Off. We make life a little easier so you can relax and enjoy your vacation! Visit our website for details on Grocery and Wine Provisioning and Gourmet Drop-Off.

Blue Sky Luxury Concierge

Visit: www.blueskyconcierge.com

Contact or Call (615) 604-2447

Blue Sky offers luxury concierge, provisioning and private event planning services for individuals, families and corporations visiting the Virgin Islands. Allow us to find the perfect rental villa or yacht for your vacation. We can plan a variety of activities such as boat charters around the Virgin Islands, sunset sails, paddle board & kayak tours, in-villa massages & chefs, dive excursions, childcare, private transportation from the St. Thomas airport to St. John, rental cars, etc. Planning a corporate retreat, incentive trip or 50th birthday party? From small intimate parties to large-scale corporate events allow Blue Sky turn your vacation and event dreams into a reality.

CPSIA information can be obtained
at www.ICGtesting.com
Printed in the USA
BVHW031908220721
612657BV00006B/77